BLACK BELT®
B·O·O·K·S

MW01149003

DOJO DYNAMICS

ESSENTIAL MARKETING PRINCIPLES FOR MARTIAL ARTS SCHOOLS

DR. JERRY BEASLEY

DOJO DYNAMICS

ESSENTIAL MARKETING PRINCIPLES FOR MARTIAL ARTS SCHOOLS

DR. JERRY BEASLEY

Edited by Sarah Dzida, Raymond Horwitz,
Jeannine Santiago and Jon Sattler

Graphic Design by John Bodine

©2009 Black Belt Communications LLC

All Rights Reserved
Printed in the United States of America
Library of Congress Control Number: 2008944224
ISBN-10: 0-89750-169-1
ISBN-13: 978-0-89750-169-9

First Printing 2009

BLACK BELT BOOKS
A Division of **OHARA [ⓤ] PUBLICATIONS, INC.**
World Leader in Martial Arts Publications

DEDICATION

I dedicate this book to my father Fred M. Beasley (1925-2003) who was a decorated U.S. Marine during World War II. He became a hero to many, most notably his three sons. Men like my father returned from Japan in the 1940s with hand-to-hand combat skills and introduced Americans to the Asian fighting arts.

ACKNOWLEDGMENTS

I want to thank Scott Yates for his advice and AIKIA.net designer John Miller for his Web expertise. I also appreciate the positive impact of professional marketers like Rob Colasanti and Stephen Oliver from the National Association for Professional Martial Artists, and Frank Silverman, David Wahl and John Corcoran from the Martial Arts Industry Association. Finally, I wish to thank *Black Belt* book editor Sarah Dzida and the professional editorial staff at *Black Belt*. Were it not for the decades of coverage afforded to martial artists by *Black Belt*, the martial arts industry might still be composed of a few former servicemen bent on privately and secretly teaching the arts.

PREFACE

In the summer of 1973, I taught a young student named Mike Marr *taekwondo* at an exclusive university sports camp in Blacksburg, Virginia. Mike was 6 years old and an eager student. He had studied taekwondo a little with one of my teachers, Soo Wong Lee, a hard-nosed master with calluses on his forehead and knuckles from breaking bricks.

At the camp graduation, I asked Mike to demonstrate some self-defense moves with me, which the audience loved. Unbeknownst to me, Mike's father, Bill Marr, was in the audience and was impressed by the performance. Following his son's demonstration, Marr, a self-made millionaire, was so inspired by Chuck Norris' appearance on *The Tonight Show Starring Johnny Carson* that he contacted Norris the next day. The two opened a Chuck Norris Karate Studio in the Janaf Shopping Center in Norfolk, Virginia.

I visited Bill Marr several times at his Chuck Norris Karate Studio in the late 1970s. Underneath his gruff professional exterior, he was a kind man, and he taught me how to develop a contract for belt programs and how to do sales and promotions. He allowed me to watch his salespeople practice their craft. He also showed me how to develop a client profile and collect on contracts.

I wrote about Marr's methods in my doctoral dissertation at Virginia Tech in 1979. In 1980, I put his program into practice by opening my own studio. The school was also the headquarters for my national martial arts organization, the American Independent Karate Instructors Association. Because of the success of the operation, I was able to partner with karate and kickboxing champion Joe Lewis, who became AIKIA's national director for training and instruction in 1983. The organization provided international rank registration, accreditation and consultation for curriculum, and marketing strategies for schools. Eventually, the organization began to take up so much of my time that I sold my karate school business and divided my time between my consulting business and teaching at Radford University in Virginia.

While the organization grew, I developed the Karate College training camp, which continues to attract top talents like Lewis, Bill Wallace and Renzo Gracie to teach each year. It also has received awards like the 2008 *Black Belt* Industry Award for Seminar/Best Training Camp. Over the years, I've teamed up with world champion and martial arts business experts like Jeff Smith, Jhoon Rhee, John Graden, Lawrence Arthur and Thom Wind to present instructor seminars at the Karate College. I have used all the wisdom that I've gained from these programs and people as the foundation for this guidebook. My sincere appreciation goes out to each of these talented individuals and especially to Bill Marr, who helped me get started.

—Dr. Jerry Beasley
2009

TABLE OF CONTENTS

PROMOTE YOUR DREAM

PROMOTE YOUR DREAM

"**I**f you build it, they will come." These inspiring words were spoken by Kevin Costner's character in *Field of Dreams*. He believed that if he built a baseball field in an Iowa cornfield, a group of baseball legends would appear. Of course, in the movie they appeared, and the film ended happily.

In real life, there are people who believe that if they build a martial arts school, run a karate club, or host a seminar or summer camp, participants will appear. Unfortunately, lack of participation has provided an unhappy ending for countless schools and organizations. Try taking out the word "build" in that famous movie quote and replace it with "market." Now you have a more realistic statement: If you market your program, students will come.

Marketing is the key to making a martial arts school, seminar or summer camp work. Quite a few years ago, I invested all my savings in my first martial arts studio. Like so many others, I thought, if I build it, they will come. The students did not come. Instead, I had to learn how to promote and market my school. I took seminars, studied books and tapes, and apprenticed myself to several successful salespeople. Eventually, I saw a return on my efforts. I not only was making better money but also was running a more successful school. My classes filled, and I soon knew it was time to expand.

As my karate business evolved into a martial arts organization, I was able to teach my marketing strategy to others across the country. I showed instructors how to build their dreams with a work ethic that helps develop the students and the school. Before signing up a new student, I told instructors to ask themselves two questions:

- Can I help this student?
- Can the student afford to pay for my instruction?

Realize that not everyone will benefit from your specific type of instruction. Suppose a young lady entering your school wanted a reality-based self-defense program, but your school only teaches *taekwondo* for Olympic-style competitions. Your goals are different: The lady wants to learn reality-based martial arts, but you only teach a competition-based art. Your school won't serve the best interest of the student. Instead of trying to sell your program to her, help her find another instructor or develop a reality-based self-defense class. Likewise, if a member of the military wanted to sign up for classes but admitted that he would be called for duty in three months, it would not be ethical to sell him a one-year contract because he would be unable to receive the services he paid for.

Remember, martial arts businesses aren't all about making money. As a martial arts professional, you have the opportunity and obligation to help potential students learn how to protect themselves, improve their physique, increase their self-esteem, create a strong identity, develop group bonds and establish character traits like discipline, perseverance and responsibility, which are admired and accepted by society at large. By helping the potential student get what he wants, whether its physical prowess or higher confidence, you will get what you want: success, money and a sense of self-worth from helping the community.

You can't get what you want until you help others get what they want.

The principles and techniques of marketing—which include developing a plan, pricing, placement, advertising, public relations, proper image and sales promotions—are used to effectively attract prospects to visit your school. Combine these skills with the art of selling and quality client services, and you have a system for success. As you get to know the prospective students and they become excited about your program, you are better able to qualify their potential or determine whether they are a good fit for your program. You also can answer the two questions: How can you help them and what can they afford?

Using the right tools—such as an introductory lesson (free or paid), a tour of the facility, introduction to the instructor, a PowerPoint presentation and a professional presentation binder—will set your school apart from others. When a prospective student is expertly evaluated, closing the deal becomes simple. The standard objections are addressed before you ask him to commit to your program. The results of tailoring your program to the needs of the prospects lead to more members, income, staff, larger facilities, additional locations and a greater benefit to the community you serve. Even more important, defining the structure and tone of the training will help your students become black belts.

As a final note, imagine purchasing a set of weights in the hopes of building muscle. To reach your goal, you must follow a weight routine at least three times a week. Some pros lift weights every day, hitting a different body part in each session. Others buy weights but fail to use them. Some use the weights a few times but are disappointed by the results and leave the weights to gather dust on a shelf.

This book and program can be likened to the weight set. It takes work and steady application to make it work for you. Every day, you must spend time updating your publicity, advertising and sales promotions. Every day, you must be able to identify new prospects for your school. Every day, you must spend time perfecting your product or service. If you let this book just sit on the shelf, nothing will happen. Work hard and good luck!

How to Read This Book

Each chapter discusses a key marketing tactic. There is a concept outline beneath each chapter title. From there, the text is generally broken up into various subsections that address these concepts. All these devices are meant to facilitate reading.

CHAPTER 2

MARTIAL ARTS AS A BUSINESS

MARTIAL ARTS AS A BUSINESS

history • evolution of the business • profit vs. passion

The practice of martial arts in the United States started small and was mostly limited to World War II veterans, who introduced it to the public upon their return from the Pacific. "Karate" became the all-encompassing buzzword for martial arts, which is why legendary *kenpo* master Ed Parker is generally acknowledged as the first person to open a commercial karate school in 1956.

By the early 1960s, former servicemen such as Mike Stone, Chuck Norris and Joe Lewis began to establish reputations as teachers and students of Asian martial arts. The popularity of karate tournaments allowed stylists to share and mix skills from the martial arts of Japan, Okinawa, Korea and China. Despite heightened popularity, karate schools remained few and far between, and making a living as a teacher of martial arts was a lifestyle that offered limited compensation.

By the late 1960s, taekwondo schools became popular in most major U.S. cities. The Korean government sponsored many taekwondo masters and helped them open *dojang*. Korean instructors worked many hours building and promoting their schools. Popular TV shows like *Kung Fu* and movies like *Billy Jack* brought new interest to martial arts programs. By 1973, the stage was set for the first national proliferation of martial arts schools.

In 1973, *Five Fingers of Death* and other popular Chinese films referred to as "chopsockies" introduced many Americans to martial arts. The most notable film was Bruce Lee's *Enter the Dragon*. Lee's untimely and unfortunate death in July of that year added to the attention now being directed toward martial arts. In the summer of 1973, martial arts schools began to open in every major city and suburb.

The boom in martial arts schools lasted little more than a year. The oil embargo of 1974 meant that many people couldn't afford recreational pursuits like the martial arts. The boom of 1973 turned into the bust of 1974, catching many instructors off-guard. With the death of Lee, the cancellation of the popular TV show *Kung Fu,* and the general recession in economic growth, the martial arts school industry took an immediate nosedive.

By the late 1970s, interest in the martial arts reignited. Norris starred in a series of successful movies. Cable sports channel ESPN began promoting full-contact karate matches. Champions like Bill "Superfoot" Wallace became mainstream sports personalities. Meanwhile, martial arts school owners noticed the renewed interest in martial arts. It wasn't long before a few enterprising martial artists discovered that they could make big money from karate and taekwondo school ownership.

The 1980s were excellent years for karate schools. Hollywood favored the industry with *The Karate Kid* and the *Teenage Mutant Ninja Turtles* film series. The seminar circuit became a much more lucrative business for promoters and performers like Wallace, Lewis, Dan Inosanto and Stephen K. Hayes. Toward the end of the decade, super-camps like Karate College sprang up. Successful entrepreneur Andrew Wood published the now-famous instructional manual on how to make a six-figure salary by teaching karate. Implementing the methods for making a $100,000, however, would not seriously take place until the 1990s.

The arrival of business organizations in the 1990s were extremely important to the development of martial arts schools. With a sizeable investment from Century Martial Arts Supply, the National Association of Professional Martial Artists was able to recruit almost 2,000 school owners and turn martial arts instruction into a billion-dollar industry. Today, NAPMA and other organizations like the Martial Arts Industry Association help martial arts instructors develop successful strategies for school instruction, marketing and management.

One of the major problems facing martial arts instructors of the past were that they didn't know how to effectively profit through martial arts instruction. The individual charged with the task of running the martial arts school assumed both the role of compassionate, trusting and humble master as well as the strong-minded, fast-talking and hard-toothed entrepreneur. Often, the roles conflicted. As a result, the instructor who could not strike a happy medium became either the poor but well-thought-of master or the well-to-do but not so respected entrepreneur.

After many years of business evolution, martial arts teachers now believe that profiting from professional business practices is not contrary to the act of shaping good martial arts students. Making more money means they can afford larger facilities and teach even more students. By using professional business practices, many qualified instructors can now work full time maintaining their art's traditions through well-structured programs and instruction.

CHAPTER

3

DEVELOP A MARKETING PLAN

DEVELOP A MARKETING PLAN

goals • targeting your audience • plan outline

A marketing plan is a strategy that details the necessary actions you must take to successfully sell your product. In the 1960s and 1970s, instructors relied on word-of-mouth advertising and publicity from martial arts movies for their marketing plan. In addition, the primary method for teaching karate-style arts could best be described as "survival of the fittest." Students were humiliated into learning "character," endured torturous physical training sessions, and couldn't train with other instructors.

For example, in 1968 the class I participated in started with 30 members. Within a few months, the group dwindled to 15. By the end of the year, only four remained. On a typical night, we exercised for 30 minutes by performing every kick and every punch up to 100 times each. We practiced the same *kata* a dozen times, and at the end of class, we sparred without protective gear for 30 minutes. Strict military-style discipline was stressed in every class. The instructor would bark out commands and strike students with a short stick if they made mistakes. If he had to correct a student more than twice, he made the class do push-ups on their knuckles. In the end, I was the only person who earned a black belt from my original school. No wonder we had a hard time getting new people to join the class. Rather than motivating students to invest their time in taking martial arts, the typical martial arts program was designed to weed out all but the top students who could endure the rigorous training.

The modern, confidence-building approach to learning self-defense attracts far more students than the traditional, disciplined approach. However, the old image still exists in many parents' minds, and this leads back to the question of any good businessman: How do I get potential students in the door?

The answer is through your marketing plan. As mentioned earlier, the first commercial martial arts instructors in the United States were often World War II veterans who had day jobs and taught karate and *jujutsu* on the side. As these Americans developed as instructors, some also learned how to market their programs successfully by tailoring them to the needs of the students. Over the last few decades, the practice of teaching, performing and marketing martial arts has become a billion-dollar industry. Those who have become the most successful had a marketing plan that worked.

Why the Concern for Martial Arts Now?

Professional martial arts marketers know how to determine what potential students and clients want. They also create pricing and distribute the products and services that clients need. These marketers use publicity, advertising, sales promotions and personal selling to recruit clients to their schools. These are the facets of their marketing plan.

Determining why prospective students would be willing to pay for your services is the foundation of your marketing plan and will shape all the decisions you make. Here are some common reasons why Americans participate in the martial arts:

Health/Fitness

Americans are increasingly overweight, which can lead to heart disease and anxiety brought about by a hurried lifestyle.

Self-Defense

Crime is on the rise. Many people will be the victims of assault. Rape is a serious problem on college campuses, and school violence, especially among young children, is a reality.

Character Development/Self-Regulation*/Self-Esteem

Family dysfunction, self-esteem issues and a sense of isolation are issues that are more visible today than ever. A martial arts school environment provides a satisfactory family unit for some and an environment where members may achieve rank, responsibility and status. The martial arts are definitely a cure for an ailing society.

Self-Image/Pop Culture

The popular image of male and female movie stars promotes fitness and martial arts. On a daily basis, Hollywood sells us buff bodies with the ability to kick butt. Animated movies, cartoons, commercials and other media efforts have used the martial arts to make their products more attractive. Popular mixed-martial arts stars have combined their buff bodies with the sports-hero image to create an unprecedented interest in martial arts competitions.

Self-regulation is an ability that children can develop. It enables them to perform tasks without immediate adult supervision.

As you can see, there is a massive need and interest in the martial arts industry, which translates to money in the bank for the successful instructor. However, you also must inspire rather than nag students and their parents to join, which is what your marketing plan will do. The martial arts school must be multidimensional: It needs to educate students about healthy living, teach them self-defense techniques, instill them with self-discipline and character, and provide a service that works while creating a social atmosphere in which students feel that they are part of a positive social group.

This all boils down to two components for a successful marketing plan:

- First, school instructors must teach a functional martial art or combination of arts in an educational, progressive and professional system or curriculum that leads to a series of goals.

- Second, school instructors must offer students a social system that encourages a sense of belonging and a commitment and desire to encourage others to join.

By successfully creating and maintaining a commonly shared belief that "this is so much fun I want to share it with others," or "this has really helped my child," the martial arts school can grow to its full potential. Failure at either level will limit the growth of the school. Your marketing plan should and will address all these concerns.

Creating the Marketing Plan

Some school owners continue to follow the old marketing plan of relying on TV and film publicity and word-of-mouth advertising as their primary method for recruiting new students. However, the modern martial arts school owner develops his or her marketing based on proven methods that serve the instructors' and students' needs.

Educating yourself is the first step to expanding your school and improving your ability to run it. I have taken many marketing courses and seminars and have read countless books. I remember that each professor would begin the semester with the marketing plan. Some would have four or five steps, while others would list more. This book will cover the core principles to opening, marketing and expanding your martial arts school. While each chapter covers a specific topic, marketing requires a broad understanding of its individual parts.

Take the time to research and develop solutions for each of the topics addressed, then put them into action in a month-by-month marketing plan.

It takes time, but it is extremely valuable to the martial arts owner who wants to build a successful business. The following five questions will help you begin to understand the dynamics of your marketing process. Develop functional answers for each.

1. How Can My Service Benefit Others?

The benefits that you offer might include a more affordable program than your competition, a cleaner and more professional location, flexible hours, or a better system of presenting your material to a new student. Is there a daytime market in your area? Perhaps your school design will be unique because it has padded mats, parent/guest seating, a pro shop, etc. Develop a studio that will suit the clientele you are trying to attract: dedicated, respectful, loyal students you can help and who can pay your fees. It is your responsibility to create that atmosphere from the start. Of course, your art, reputation or notoriety might help attract students, as well.

To better understand your market and your competition, visit other schools. Collect all published materials from competing clubs. Study the successful clubs' advertisements, Yellow Pages listings and so on. Research the competitions' strengths and weaknesses. Discover how you can be unique in your market and offer benefits to your customers.

2. What Is the Target Market?

Consider the different martial arts styles being taught today. Judo tends to be for people who like to grapple in uniforms. Taekwondo is usually geared for kids because they can more easily develop the flexibility required for the advanced kicks. Mixed-martial arts programs are perhaps best intended for young adults who can withstand the rigorous conditioning and contact required for competition. Karate is the well-known name of an art that can be taught to children, adults and seniors. Kickboxing can either attract a large fitness crowd or, if it involves competition and knockouts, frighten off more timid members. Once you identify what public image you want to project, you can better understand how that image will attract certain prospects.

To do this, develop a product profile by researching income levels, age groups and other demographics in the immediate area where you plan to open a school. The information will show you the potential consequences of your marketing decision. For example, if you open your school in a low-rent district, chances are you will attract lower-income members. You may still draw in good students, but you will need to consider whether they can afford to pay the prices that you desire. Many of the more successful full-time schools are located in shopping areas. Prices are higher, but the potential market can offset the higher overhead costs of rent, utilities, etc. Your product profile will help you decide where to locate your school.

3. How Will I Advertise My School?

Are you targeting lower- or higher-income students? Your location might provide the answer to this question. It could be that in your community, the wealthy read certain periodicals or frequent certain locations.

A friend of mine markets personal black-belt programs to a select clientele. He charges $15,000 per year for the program. His clients are wealthy. He advertises through word of mouth, but he belongs to city business clubs and meets with clients through business luncheons.

If you want to be successful, start making these decisions in advance. Organize your advertising campaign into monthly or seasonal intervals. For most martial arts schools, business starts to pick up in September (when kids go back to school). January and February are the traditional heavy recruitment months for most fitness and martial arts programs. Many people make New Year's resolutions to get fit, learn something new, meet new friends or learn self-defense. Advertising at this time of the year is the most effective.

There is often a wave of new sign-ups around March and April because people want to get in shape for the summer. And summer is often the low point for signing long-term contracts. Use this information to develop an advertising budget. Spend money during peak recruitment times and limit expenditures during weak months.

4. How Will I Finance My School and Its Programs?

It's time to develop a budget. Determine a close estimation of how much money you expect to make weekly, monthly and annually. Figure in the costs of construction, maintenance, supplies, equipment and other necessities, then determine what percentage will be taken from gross sales, which I'll discuss in a moment.

If you plan to borrow startup money from a bank, have a business plan that details your expenses. A mentor—like someone who operates a successful school—is a good source of information. If you are developing your own plan and accumulated some price estimates, begin to organize these costs into a month-by-month business plan.

Start by determining the potential value of each student. Let's say you are located in a small shopping center and you have priced your programs at $100 per month. A single student pays $1,200 per year in basic tuition. Each new student pays a $100 initiation fee. You charge a belt-testing fee of $40 per exam, and each student takes three exams per year ($120 per student for testing fees). Each student spends $500 (during the year) at your pro shop for items such as uniforms, DVDs, sparring gear and weapons. Adding the expenses ($1,200+$100+$120+$500= $1,920), you have a conservative estimated value of $1,920 per student.

Yearly Program Value Per Student
$ 1,200 Basic Tuition
$ 100 Initiation Fee
$ 120 ($40 x 3) Belt-Testing Fee
+ 500 Other Expenses
TOTAL $1,920 Yearly Program Value

You have a nice school, a charismatic instructor and a popular program. You provide an excellent service to each member. You are located next to an elementary school and a shopping center in a community of at least 80,000 people. You plan to perform weekly demos at places like school physical-education classes, business organizations and malls. And you plan to put up fliers and have a lead-box promotion each month. (For more on this promotion, see Page 104.) You coordinate the fliers and boxes with the demos. Each demo attracts three visitors to your school, and one signs up for a year of instruction. From the 50 demos, you sign up 50 students. Your students like your class so much that each student will eventually account for one new student. You now have 50 original students and 50 new students brought in by word of mouth. By the end of your first year, you have 100 members in your school. A class of 100 with a student value of $1,920 each yields a yearly gross income of $192,000!

Yearly Gross Income
$1,920 Approximate Program Value Per Year
x   100 Number of Students in Program
TOTAL $192,000 Yearly Gross Income

However, your yearly net income or salary would be $89,000. To get there, you pay $4,000 per month in rent and utilities. To furnish your school with top-quality mats, target training gear and other accommodations, you pay another $2,000 per month. This amount also includes the cost of your pro shop. You make back much of this money in student value. The cost of phones, printing, Web site maintenance, travel (to work and to demos) averages $1,000 per month. You budget $19,000 for advertising because experts recommend that you spend 10 percent of your gross income on it. Add the $48,000 ($4,000 x 12) in rent, $24,000 ($2,000 x 12) in accommodations, $12,000 ($1,000 x 12) in general promotions and $19,000 in advertising for a total expenditure of $103,000 for the first year. Your school brought in gross receipts of $192,000. You spent $103,000.

Yearly Net Income
$192,000 Yearly Gross Income
$ 48,000 Program rental Space and Utilities
$ 24,000 Space Expenses and Upkeep
$ 19,000 Advertising
- 12,000 General Promotions
TOTAL $ 89,000 Yearly Net Income

Keep in mind that the gross and net incomes were based on 100 students paying all fees during the entire year. You may have only 30 students the first few months. You need about 60 students (at a value of $1,920 per student) to pay the bills. I offer these figures just to get you started on developing your own plan. Take some time and figure all the possibilities.

5. How Do I Promote My School?

You know the products and services that you offer, so you can identify your target market and prospective clientele. You also have an advertising strategy and a business plan that details your budget. The fifth part of the marketing plan is to identify specific promotions. The goal is to coordinate the tools or promotional methods you use to advertise, publicize and sell your theme, whether it's fitness, self-defense or another topic.

There are four components to the promotional process: advertising, publicity, sales promotions and personal selling. Advertising informs and educates the public by letting people know the location of your school, your offerings and why they need your services. While you usually have to pay for advertising space to have your school appear in a newspaper, you may attract the attention of an editor who will write a story about an accomplishment you have made. This publicity, which is used to attract attention, doesn't cost any money and builds a positive reputation for your school. Sales promotions are best thought of as incentives that bring in new prospects. Sales promotions are covered in Chapter 7 and includes ideas such as "two-for-one sign-up fees" and martial arts-themed birthday parties. By using advertising, public relations and sales promotions, you will attract new people to your club. Once the students are in your class, use personal selling to assist them in signing a contract. The book will address all these components in later chapters.

Changing Your Marketing Plan

As you gain experience in marketing, you will adapt and change your marketing plan because of market trends or changing times. For example, while newspaper and directory advertising has been a focal point for schools during the 20th century, today's martial arts marketers rely on Internet sites and cell phones. Instructors have also changed the way they teach, and they follow "user-friendly" lesson plans that stress fun, fitness and self-defense rather than rough, militaristic discipline. School owners have made major marketing inroads in earning the attention of high-income executives with fitness kickboxing programs and personalized black-belt options, as well as with children's self-defense and activity programs.

Each of the sections outlined in the marketing plan must be thoroughly researched and applied because change in student numbers can translate to a significant difference in loss or gain. To ensure that your school will remain in the profit column, you must carefully plan and also meticulously carry out the plan. Running a martial arts school takes a lot of hard work. Expect to work 60-hour weeks and, if you love what you do, expect to enjoy every minute you devote to attaining and maintaining your dream.

The next chapter will explain how to create your product, how to price it and where to locate your studio.

CHAPTER 4

PRODUCT, PLACEMENT
AND PRICING

PRODUCT, PLACEMENT AND PRICING

*curriculum • martial arts organizations • ranks • finding a perfect location
facilities • making competitive pricing • obtaining capital*

Every marketing student knows the four "P's": **product** (your martial art), **placement** (the location of your school), **price** (how much you charge for instruction) and **promotion** (how you let others know about your school and get them to join). Promotion is further divided into the categories of advertising, publicity, sales promotions and personal selling. Once you learn these methods, you will employ them to get students to join your class.

Most martial arts business owners spend the majority of their time developing the product, which in this case refers is their art or style. But even if you are a master teacher or world champion athlete, you still need to learn how to properly price your program. You must learn where to best locate your school and how to use tools such as advertising and publicity to promote your programs. If you fail to master the principles of marketing, your success will be greatly limited. Think of the marketing plan as your blueprint to success. The four P's represent the ways you will carry out your plan.

P1: Product

Martial arts business owners sell a product and offer a service. While the product might include uniforms, safety gear and other equipment as well as certifications, the primary product that they offer—martial arts training—isn't something tangible that can be put in a box.

For example, while the fitness club owner might sell the concept of being fit, he cannot sell 20-inch biceps and a 30-inch waist to his potential customers. Rather, the club owner sells a process to achieve those results. Similarly, the martial arts school owner sells a concept. He provides students with a documented and measured program that leads to the goals discussed in the previous chapter, like bully-proofing kids, adult self-defense and character development. Martial arts business owners' products and services tend to improve fitness, self-discipline, confidence, self-esteem and a person's overall feeling of accomplishment. In short, these characteristics and attributes are necessary for success in sports, self-defense and life. Another added benefit is that the product occurs in a wholesome family environment in which lasting friendships are made.

Developing a Product/Service That Works

When developing your product, you need the right mix of what to teach and how to teach it. This takes time. Variables like teaching style, organization membership and ranking procedures may vary from school to school. It's important to make sure that your school has the correct elements for whatever concept you plan to market. For example, if your school teaches mixed martial arts, you must have a cage, training equipment, curriculum plans and a facility that will accommodate the students in their quest to become MMA champions. If your school is all about an ancient tradition, its design should reflect proper feng shui and be decorated like a traditional *dojo*, while the curriculum should stress kata and the reasoning behind it, which is known as *bunkai*.

To sell your intangible product, you must also be a teacher. And to become a teacher, you must first think like a student. By knowing what and how students learn and comprehend in different types of classes, teachers can better develop their programs to assist the students' growth. To master the art of teaching, put yourself in the role of each student, including the fast learner, the slow learner and the special-needs learner; the master teacher is forever the student.

In this regard, teaching methods are important because a martial arts instructor must have an effective program that can be shown to prospective students. It must offer concrete opportunities to measure your students' advancement. To help all your students reach their individual goals, present your lessons in a variety of ways. Most educators have four distinct methods for delivering information:

Hands-On Instruction

In most schools, the majority of a student's time is spent rehearsing techniques, drills, etc. In order to facilitate learning, the student must perform the skills to the best of his ability and in a manner that resembles the act that he intends to perform. Free-form sparring with safety gear represents the most realistic form of hands-on expression. The student should graduate into sparring instruction carefully because beginners aren't ready for it. Rather, the student should gradually learn to perform the move and positions and apply the skills. To get to the hands-on level, the student must have adequate instruction covering the other three methods in this chart.

Simulated Experience

"Simulated experience" encourages the student to go through the motions of a desired goal in order to prepare for the actual experience. A step down from free-form sparring, simulated experience may include focus-pad drills and two-man self-defense drills. Simulated-experience drills are also among the most easily controlled ad popular methods of instruction. I personally recommend that simulated-experience drills become a major part of the class routine.

Dramatization

As the third method of instruction, dramatization is used to act out self-defense techniques by striking an imaginary opponent. Kata is an example of dramatization because the student pantomimes a real fight by kicking and punching the air or performs a skill without a partner or training aid. Keep in mind that there exists a rank, or order, for the different training methods. Often, you hear that dramatic kata is an excellent training method for self-defense. Dramatization is a less efficient method for developing combat skills. Imagine a person who performs a weightlifting kata. Can he develop the same muscle size as the person who actually uses weights? To become proficient at combat, you must engage in hands-on practices like sparring or grappling. You may develop a mental image of being successful through rigorous and repeated kata practice. In many cases, however, students simply go through the motions mindlessly, getting little more than exercise from kata practice.

Demonstration/Explanation

A fourth method of instruction is the demonstration/explanation. The instructor simply demonstrates a technique and then explains what he has done. The instructor should keep in mind that demonstration/explanation can be enhanced by following up with a dramatization and then a high-stress exercise, such as hard-contact sparring. Again, you are advised to consider the intended result and then select training skills to meet those goals.

Developing a theme for your school—such as self-defense, sparring or art—will help you create lesson plans that reflect your public image and give you the best results. Remember, you will find many martial arts schools in any neighborhood. Creating a unique identity helps you develop the reputation as the best school in your market for your specific style.

For example, a martial arts school owner who advertises realistic self-defense training—now called reality training—prepares students for high-risk contact with sparring and scenario training. An owner who focuses on the cultural aspects of karate or taekwondo might promote the practice of kata through dramatization. The important thing to remember is that the method of delivery can influence the outcome. The mark of a successful school can be measured in the overall preparedness of the students.

If you are planning a seminar or summer camp, you should understand how to deliver your lessons clearly. The successful seminar performer will devote less time to lecture and more time to getting the participants involved in simulated-experience drills. Similarly, successful summer camps are filled with stimulating activities.

Organizing a School Curriculum

Your students' needs are met primarily through instruction, which is a large part of your product. In some cases, it may be that your school identity becomes linked with the idea that you teach a classical style that is unaltered and unchanged from its original form. This may be a selling point. Entrepreneurial teachers often develop a chain or franchise identity, which allows them to teach their curriculum to other instructors through videos or seminars. Most school instructors today have earned their black belts in a "modernized" form of a classical art. They are used to mixing arts and typically prefer to stay abreast of new, innovative and popular additions to their martial arts curriculums. Some school instructors create a niche market based on the fact that they offer multiple styles instead of a single one.

In the chart provided on the following page, you can better understand the focus of your program by identifying the percentage of time you will devote to each task.

Understanding Your Curriculum Objectives
Please fill in each section.

Objectives

My primary objective is to promote:

Self-Defense   _____%

Sport/Competition   _____%

Character Development   _____%

Fitness   _____%

     TOTAL 100%

The primary methods of training used in my school include:

Lecture/Demonstration   _____%

Kata (Dramatization)   _____%

Basic Techniques and Drills, Air (Dramatization)   _____%

Bunkai (Dramatization)   _____%

One-Step or Controlled Sparring   _____%

Focus-Pad Drills (Simulated Experience)   _____%

Point Sparring (Hands-On Experience)   _____%

Contact Sparring (Hands-On Experience)   _____%

     TOTAL 100%

If your school focuses on self-defense and your primary teaching method uses kata and striking the air, you may need to rethink your curriculum plan. According to Bruce Lee, self-defense is "spontaneous and unrehearsed," and many combat trainers agree with Lee on this point. Contrary to the flow of real combat, kata and prearranged self-defense practice is organized and rehearsed. You know exactly what the other person is supposed to do and you react to the skills accordingly. Many of the new reality-training and performance-based combative instructors use sparring, rolling and other contact training as their primary teaching method because they believe that the student must practice drills that are as close to the chaos and spontaneity expected in a real street fight.

If your student body is composed mostly of kids and your primary goal is to develop disciplined citizens, kata and traditional drills may be a perfect match. By charting your preferred teaching methods, you are able to better evaluate your teaching curriculum and develop a method that best meets the needs of your clientele. Equally important, you become better able to organize your marketing strategy, publicity campaign and advertising to reach your target market.

The professional teacher must constantly evaluate and update teaching methods and curriculum. Why? Because the martial arts market constantly changes. To increase productivity, be aware of changes in students' needs and understand how to best meet those needs.

Awarding Belt Ranks

The process of awarding belt ranks plays an important part in shaping your product's identity because they give students concrete incentives to be involved in your program. Most styles use a belt system based on three to nine belt colors and 10 student ranks ranging from the beginning 10th *kyu*/*gup*/grade to the advanced first grade. The 10th grade is the white belt. Levels nine, eight and seven are typically yellow, gold and orange. The sixth, fifth and fourth grades are the intermediate ranks and are often identified with the green, blue and purple colors. The senior-student ranks include levels three, two and one and are most often identified with the brown, red and black belts.

A student who is practicing a minimum of two hours per week may advance in belt rank every three or four months. This means that an average student may move through the student ranks in about 27 to 30 months. Many school owners with a large student enrollment of kids younger than 12 often include two or more extra ranks to provide additional learning experiences for preschool-age children. While one school owner may use hash marks or stripes to determine rank, another school owner may prefer to award a different belt color per new rank. When a student completes the last color belt, he may test for first *dan* within three to six months. The process from 10th-grade white belt to first-degree black is expected to take three years.

Once a student advances to the dan level, he comes under a new standard for promotions. In the traditional concept of dan rank, a student could advance to the next dan level only after sufficient time-in-grade was achieved. Typically, it takes two years to advance from first dan to second dan, three years to move from second dan to third dan, four years to advance from third dan to fourth dan, and five years to advance from fourth dan to fifth dan. While dan ranks, including first through third, are awarded for excellence in skill, the fourth and fifth dans are awarded in part for teaching expertise. (Skill is expected to continue at an exemplary level.) This process may vary widely from school to school and from one organization to another.

The dan ranks represented by the sixth, seventh and eighth dan are master instructor ranks reserved for professionals who have made teaching a career and have produced a large number of skilled black belts. There is the expectation that the recipient of such an advanced rank will serve five or more years of time-in-grade before the next level of advancement. Finally, the levels of ninth and 10th dan are reserved for the few professional martial artists who have spent 40 to 50 years teaching and promoting black belts to master level. To become a "grandmaster," you must first produce master-level students. Most advanced ranks are certified by an organization.

Organizations

Should you join a martial arts organization? If you feel strongly that your style contains all the information you need, joining a style organization may be a good choice. In addition, because they have ready-made markets, organizations can help you better recruit for your programs, seminars or summer camps.

Most organizations tend to restrict their training to skills and procedures that have been dictated by the style's founder or head. Some organizations—like the American Taekwondo Association and World Taekwondo Federation—have been in business for more than 30 years and are considered leading choices for school memberships.

Organizations like AIKIA cater to the concept of "independent" styles that allow the instructors to choose, learn and mix aspects from additional styles. Both the restricted- and independent-style organizations have merit, which is why it's important to identify which approach best fits your interest before committing to the organization. There is always an advantage to offering your students national accreditation by the organization. You just have to decide whether the cost of membership is of value to you in the long run.

Because organizations offer teaching curriculum, continuing education, instructor certification and student accreditation, shop around and find out who the organizations' chief instructors are before joining one. After all, you may end up taking lessons from the chief instructor. Also, learn what the organization expects from you. I joined a large TKD organization in the early 1970s that required that each student pay a membership and testing fee. It also required me to pay for a regional master to come to my studio and test my students. I had no idea that I was getting into that level of financial commitment. Ask for prices, including sign-up fees for students, testing fees and dan-rank fees. Call the head office and ask to speak with the chief instructor. Most instructors plan to join an organization for life, so be sure you feel completely comfortable with the association you choose.

Styles

Is there a particular martial art or method that attracts the most participants? Conventional wisdom suggests that kids and their parents will join karate and taekwondo schools while 18- to 30-year olds are more interested in participating in MMA instruction, fitness kickboxing, or a mixture of several arts with a focus on self-defense and fitness.

While the style you choose may initially draw attention and new students, once you are established in your community, your reputation becomes your main source of recruitment.

Should you develop your own style? The simple answer is no. A new style is born only after three generations of black belts have been produced in that style. Why three generations? Think of it like this: You decide to abandon your traditional style and develop your own style. You teach your students the new style up to the level of black belt. In order for the style to endure, your black-belt students must teach their students an unmodified version of your style up to the black-belt level. Their students must then teach their students up to the black-belt level without changing your original style, too. Once your students understand that you have, with justification, changed the original style, they will most likely use the same justification to change the style you teach them. As a result, few new styles last beyond the first generation of students and therefore qualify only as modified versions of an original style. It is indeed difficult to come up with a style that will endure the three-generation test of time.

The problem with abandoning a traditional style and creating a new style is that students will lack accreditation and recognition outside your immediate school. The best advice is to maintain the root, or base, art. If you practice karate, then maintain and market your school with the name karate. Call it "American karate," "nonclassical karate," "freestyle karate," etc. Use the same approach with other arts, such as taekwondo and *hapkido*.

Positive Mental Attitude

Among the most important virtues is a positive mental attitude. Martial arts schools of the 1960s and even the 1970s were known mostly for their instructors' negative attitudes. A compliment was hard to come by. Students were at times humiliated, made to scrub floors, struck with harmful blows and generally abused. Today, modern martial arts school owners have effectively abandoned the old traditions of student abuse. Successful school owners maintain and promote a positive mental attitude in classes.

Positive mental attitude or "mental karate" is a product that you can offer your students and it costs nothing. Too often, martial arts instructors believe that all they can offer their students are the necessary strikes, blocks and counters to survive a physical assault. However, what they fail to realize is that their students are constantly being "attacked" with negative thoughts. They are bombarded by negative thoughts on the highway, in the newspapers and on television. Over the course of a day, people fill their mind with negative thoughts: "They won't like my class," "My kick is not fast enough" or "My opponent is too advanced for me." It takes a strong, well-conditioned and positive mind-set to combat the army of negative thoughts that confront you, and this is one way that your product can help.

Martial arts instructors can employ "mental karate" to help their students maintain a positive outlook on life. By using "mental karate," students can cancel out negative thoughts before they have a chance to multiply. Practice positive mental attitudes in the way you teach, the way you talk and the way you respond to others. Keep things positive in your school. Serve as a positive role model.

Evaluating Your Product

At most progressive schools, the curriculum and teaching methods are constantly being re-evaluated. It is important to try new ideas. What happens if you decide that a skill, technique or kata that you have used for years needs to be replaced to assist your students in developing the results they need? In each case, test the new method or skill during class. If you decide to delete a skill from your traditional style, examine the effects of its removal in the teaching process for at least three months. If your addition or deletion proves valid, then maintain it for six months before re-evaluating your decision. Be open to change, try new methods, investigate new ideas, test your innovations and vow to better yourself, your teaching system and your product.

P2: Placement

You have probably heard the phrase "location, location, location." Marketing experts use it to emphasize how important proper product placement can be to the success of a business. The location or placement of your school often dictates the prices that you charge and the number of students you attract. Studies show that fitness and martial arts club participants prefer to join schools located within a three- to five-mile radius of their home or place of employment. If you locate your school in a high-income neighborhood or shopping center, you most likely will attract students from high-income families. If you locate your school in a low-income and high-crime area, your clientele will be limited to students within that immediate area.

Like other successful businesses, martial arts trainers must offer the right product at the right price in the right location. If you are planning to open a school for the first time, you should consider several factors. Visit other schools and consider their locations, the facility design and their curriculum before finalizing your plans.

Facilities

There's a popular saying in the promotional business: "You never get a second chance to make a first impression." When prospects visit your school, they come for a reason. Perhaps they need self-defense instruction. Maybe they are out of shape and need your assistance getting in shape. Upon their first visits, you have the opportunity to "turn them on" or get them excited about martial arts. Or you may inadvertently "turn them off." Having a quality facility that appears inviting is an important part of winning them over.

When searching out a site for your school, try to find a space large enough to comfortably teach a reasonable number of students (including group and private lessons). Remember, your income is limited to some extent by the number of students you can teach. I remember that my first school was built to my specifications. To both save on rent and get a preferred location, I elected to limit my mat space and increase the size of the changing rooms and lobby. In a few short months, I had to reduce the size of the changing rooms and lobby to increase my teaching space. When I was able to double the size of my teaching space, I doubled the number of students in the class. Here are some do's and don'ts that may assist you in designing the right facility:

First impressions are important to prospective clients.

A clean, well-lit and attractively decorated area is more appealing than a space with dirty toilets, rolled up mats, unpainted walls, a musty odor or a cluttered desk.

Do as much of the remodeling as possible yourself.

At minimum, use a partition to separate the workout area from the office. In your office, you will be doing your sales presentation to recruit new students and sign contracts. You don't want class noise to interfere with your sales presentation, and you don't want other students listening to the way you sign up new students. (See Page 130.)

Provide a viewing area, preferably with one-way mirrors for parents and guests.

Separating students from visitors can be very important. You want students to depend on you for assignments and not be distracted by their parents. Some parents think they have to coach their kids from the sidelines, which often distracts the instructor and other students. Additionally, prospective clients might gain more of an appreciation of what your program offers by privately viewing a class.

Include large mirrors in the workout area.

Instructors may benefit from watching their students while they demonstrate skills in front of the class. Students may compare their stances and skills to other students in the mirror without turning their body.

Provide adequate lighting in all facilities.

Having your facility well lit inside and out helps in several ways. Students are affected positively by good lighting. A poorly lit classroom does not create excitement. Good lighting outside the studio helps attract attention and limits undesirable behavior.

Try to locate your facility in a high-traffic zone.

It makes sense that if more people pass by your studio, you will have more opportunities to present your product to the public. This is an example of why product and placement are so interdependent.

Convenience and Visibility

America is the land of fast food. People don't want to take a lot of time to get something done. Place your program in a convenient and easy-to-locate facility and you increase the likelihood of success. In an age of increased gas prices and adverse traffic conditions, convenience becomes a major factor in selecting a location. Keep in mind that kids' classes tend to be offered during rush-hour traffic. Parents may choose not to drive long distances to martial arts classes. As mentioned earlier, studies show that a majority of customers prefer to shop within a three- to five-mile radius of their home. Martial arts studios located near a public school, a high-income neighborhood or a high-traffic shopping center may have the best opportunity for initial success.

Locations with high drive-by counts will naturally allow more potential members to see your club. Ask this simple question: What do you want prospects to see as they drive by your studio? Placing trophies in the window indicates that your school competes. Consider placing attractive merchandise like T-shirts, books and videos. Remember the maxim, "You sell what you show." A video player that loops footage of your class and demonstrations can attract a lot of attention.

A Note on Obtaining the Capital to Develop Your Location

The amount of money you will need varies depending on the size and location of your school. The instructor who operates from a home garage will spend less money than the individual who builds a stand-alone business from the ground up. The big problem with money is how to acquire it. There are three primary ways to gather funds:

• Finance the operation yourself with money you have accumulated. Consider family investments if it won't cause unnecessary emotional stress.

• Enlist the finances of a partner (silent or active). Occasionally, an adult student or a parent of a student will be able to provide financing.

• Borrow from a bank or loan company. Both require proper credit information. You may prefer to apply for a small-business administration loan.

Before acquiring the money to start a business, do your research. All potential lenders should be considered and all possibilities exhausted to guarantee the best deal. Also, a prior history of teaching success and a ready-made clientele (perhaps from several courses offered in the community) could influence the lender's decision.

P3: Pricing

Now that you have developed a martial arts school as your product and placed it in a profitable area, it's time to establish pricing. Several variables must be considered when setting your price, including the area, demographics, surrounding rent values and general business costs. The skill level of the instructors, their professional demeanor, the reputation of the school, and the quality of the facility also must be considered.

According to statistics provided by AIKIA, schools located in smaller towns and cities charge between $75 and $100 per month, while schools in larger cities and metropolitan areas average closer to $150 to $200 per month. Full-time instructors are expected to use a contract, called a promissory note (promise to pay). Contracts may begin on a semester system (renewed every four months), advance to a six- to 12-month contract, or include a belt system in which students agree to pay a certain amount per belt level. If the instructor elects to use a belt system, monthly payments typically are reduced for the purchase of an advanced belt contract.

A student (or parent of a student) may "cash out" the contract (pay cash to complete payment for the contract) by writing a check for the entire amount during the contract signing. The student may choose a monthly payment plan. The monthly rates are determined by the number of months needed to fulfill the contract, including a minimal down payment of the first month's instruction fee.

Some school owners include a special introductory program, such as "one month of instruction and a uniform for only $99." Others include ample sparring gear, a uniform and instruction for the $99 introductory fee. Still other school owners may find that an introductory fee of $39 or less works as an attention getter. Chapter 7 and Chapter 8 will cover this topic more thoroughly.

P4: Promotions

You must promote your school. Even if a school has the best equipment and instructors in the nation, it won't attract any students if no one knows it exists. Promotion can be broken down into four areas: advertising, public relations, sales promotions and personal selling. This book is primarily about the fourth "P" in the marketing mix, identified simply as promotions. The next chapter will examine the ways martial arts marketers have employed the art of advertising to increase their school enrollment and seminar attendance.

CHAPTER

5

ADVERTISING

ADVERTISING

fundamentals • mediums • design • successful examples

A dvertising is a form of paid communication. Because you are purchasing ad space or commercial time, you want to get the most for your money.

To illustrate this point, I spoke with two school owners. One utilizes his advertising investment wisely: He budgets $3,000 per month for paid advertising and has more than 400 students. The other believes that paid advertising is burdensome. Rather than investing in future advertisements, he is paying off the advertising debt that he accumulated the year before. As a result, he has 40 students currently enrolled. Clearly, it's important to think about how you advertise. You must match the medium, the message and the market in order to get the most from your advertising investment.

In order to succeed in your martial arts school market, approach advertising like you would approach training for competition. Becoming a champion competitor requires investing long hours in cardio exercise, nutrition selection, weight training, sparring and mental preparation. Similarly, winning your market requires investing sufficient time in advertising, public relations, sales promotions and personal selling. In both areas, training for competition and investing time in marketing your school, daily effort improves your odds for success. With that in mind, the purpose of advertising is threefold:

Provide information to the reader.

Because bigger ads are more expensive, you must make your message simple and direct. Incorporate words that are familiar to the reader, and tailor your message for the beginner, not the master. Many novice business owners mistakenly develop a message to impress their competitors rather than their customers. Instead, use your ad space to inform potential beginners. List your location, contact information, hours of operation, what to expect, etc.

Develop a favorable image of your school.

Use a quality photograph that attracts attention. Make sure all the words in your ad are spelled correctly and any numbers, such as your telephone number or pricing, are correct.

Persuade prospective clients into favorable actions.

Your ad should motivate prospective clients to contact you. To inspire them, use expressions like "offer ends soon," "you must act fast," or simply put a closing date on the offer. You could also include a coupon that the reader can bring to the studio.

Message and Spokesperson

In advertising, always sell "the sizzle, not the stink." That means emphasizing the benefits of the end result, such as the pride of owning a black belt and being physically fit. Don't sell the hard work, the long hours or the cuts and bruises. When making your ad, ask yourself: Have I created an image that will yield a favorable result?

Because martial arts school owners sell an intangible product, which is a dream or image, prospects need to be able to identify with your offer and visualize themselves as the people in your ad. If they don't, your ad will be ignored. To inspire potential customers, your ad's message and spokesperson should create an attractive image of your product that people can identify with.

First, determine the message you want your ad to convey. An excellent and productive ad—once used by the former Chuck Norris Karate Studio in Norfolk, Virginia—contained the message, "Give your child an extra chance." The ad featured an image of Norris (as the spokesman) kneeling beside a child in a karate uniform. The message offered parents a program that would help their children set goals, get in shape, build character and respect their parents. What parent wouldn't be attracted to such a message?

Picking the right spokesperson (the person featured in your ad) is important. Before choosing whom you want to include, decide who your target audience is and how the ad will appeal to them—your marketing plan should help determine what kind of spokesperson you need. Then decide what the spokesperson will say and how you want to present him or her to the public. If you use your students, should they be wearing their uniforms? Do you want to show a picture of a high-level martial artist like a black belt? Or will you show men and women working out?

I once ran an ad in a community newspaper that displayed a picture of a small boy. Two large kids stood next to him, and his books and bicycle lay on the ground. The accompanying message read: "Fear. It's something we don't want to talk about. Abandoned playgrounds, footsteps, bullies.

You can't always be there to protect your child. Give him the power of karate." The ad was effective because the message, image and spokesperson resonated with my target audience: parents. In fact, I would run this advertisement every September for the entire month.

Another ad I created was effective in college newspapers. The spokesperson wore a *gi* and black belt and stood beneath the words, "The Black Belt: A Symbol of Achievement." The ad was effective because the message and spokesperson emphasized the prestige of earning a black belt, which is extremely attractive to college students seeking status, certification and diplomas.

Ad Medium

Choosing the right medium is just as important as choosing the right message and spokesperson. A medium is a format for sharing information with a large group of people. Some examples are newspapers, magazines, radio, television and the Internet. Together, they make up the media. Take a moment to consider how you can reach prospective clients. For example, some instructors overlook newspapers because many believe that only "older" people read them. But newspapers are still one of the most useful formats for catching the eye of a parent or grandparent. Design your ads with this in mind.

If you come across an ad that has been used over and over again, it's most likely because the ad works, so research successful ads when creating a winning one of yourself. Remember, repetition is essential to getting your ad recognized by readers. Some experts say that the average reader ignores two out of three ads. You might have to run your ad several times before your target market readily identifies your message and spokesperson.

Ad Design

Remember to consult with ad representatives when putting your ads together. Ad reps track down advertising for a publication, so you will have to talk with them if you want to place an ad. Because their publication may have a graphic artist who can transform your ideas into an effective ad, it's always better to ask. It might also be a good idea to hire a freelance graphic artist to design your print ads before taking them to the publication. Do not leave it up to the ad rep to make your ad because that person may not know what your interests are. Take control of your ad design by telling the rep what you want.

Rather than paying an advertising agency to build your ads, consider purchasing pre-designed ads from popular martial arts consulting firms. There are several martial arts organizations like AIKIA that have become successful because their advice and materials work. If I were starting a school, I would join a martial arts business organization and a martial arts collection group. The collection company collects the monthly payments after you send the firm your student contracts. Having a company collect tuition saves you a lot of time and headaches. Some examples of martial arts business organizations and collection groups are MAIA, NAPMA, the Martial Arts Teachers Association, the Premier Management Group,

ASF International, Martial Arts Marketing Network, Educational Funding Co. and Easy Pay.

When designing your ad, always have a dominant focal point like those shown here. Visuals often attract more attention than words, so use a photo or illustration in each ad. Consider combining color with an unusual ad size (1 inch by 4 inches, for example). You might be able to attract attention without having to pay more for a larger ad. You might be able to select a border that will separate your ad from others on the page. Many media companies have media kits, which include ad prices, deadlines and specifications for building your ad. If the publication

offers a media kit, request one and read about what they can offer you. Research, experiment, track every ad, and ask callers and visitors how they heard about your school.

Also, make sure your ad contains your phone number, address and other pertinent information, such as your Web site or e-mail address. You may want to experiment with placing your Web site's address as the focal point of the ad.

Testimonials

Testimonials are one of the most effective methods used in successful ads. An oft-used ad design features a testimonial from a parent, such as the following: "My son was constantly the victim of bullying at school until he signed up at American Martial Arts. Now he has developed more friends and the skills to protect himself."

While kids and their parents provide excellent testimonials, consider requesting a statement from a police officer, professional athlete, judge, public-school teacher or prominent businessperson who attends your school. These professionals are trusted by their communities, which make them excellent spokespersons. Along with their brief testimonial that explains why he or she chose or like your program, include a picture of the person. Remember, any testimonial should complement your marketing plan.

How Much to Spend

From my experience, owners of schools with large enrollments (300 students or more) tend to spend $1,000 or more per month in print advertisements, while owners of small schools (less than 100 students) usually spend little or no money on newspaper advertisements. When you invest your money properly, it's just a fact that the more money you spend, the more students you'll have.

Oftentimes, larger schools have grown to that size because owners have tailored their message for the right audience in the right newspapers. As a result, they can now spend $12,000 a year on newspaper and other print advertisements. On the other hand, many owners of smaller schools give up on advertising too soon or fail to create ads that elicit favorable responses. One instructor told me, "My school is too poor to afford advertisements and too poor not to be advertising." You don't want to be in that position. Instead, you have to figure out the right size, design, message and price for your ad in whatever medium you choose.

Newspapers

Before the introduction of the Internet, newspaper advertising was considered essential to the success of any commercial school. In fact, it remains a main source of advertising for martial arts businesses.

A primary goal of newspaper advertising is to get prospective clients to visit your school. Many school owners use newspaper advertising to raise awareness about their schools or inform prospective clients about clubs or special events. Including special offers such as free lessons or discount coupons in your newspaper ads are a great way to attract prospects to your school. Regardless of your goals, the ads won't be successful if no one notices them, so use photos, testimonials and other creative means to catch the attention of prospective clients and elicit a favorable image of your school.

Newspaper ads are also popular among schools because they are easy to develop. Every newspaper has an ad manager that will take the time to help you develop an ad that gets a favorable response. Newspaper ad reps want their ads to be effective so that advertisers will continue to do business with their publication. But until you discover an ad that works for you, avoid contracts that require you to make an upfront payment in exchange for multiple ad spots.

Newspaper advertisements often work best during specific seasons. Most new-student business occurs during the "back to school" months of September and October and during the "New Year's resolution" period of January and February.

Traditionally, summer is the worst season to attract new students, but it's worth posting advertisements for martial arts summer camps in May and June if you use them in conjunction with other forms of publicity, such as press releases and word of mouth. In general, advertising captions including "free coupon," "limited enrollment" or "sign up now" are particularly effective.

Persuade the ad rep to place your ad near the lifestyle/entertainment or movie listings in the newspaper because this is where your ad will most likely receive maximum exposure. If this isn't possible, shoot for entertainment or current-events sections. You may have to pay more for guaranteed ad placement, but in most cases, it will be worth the extra cost. Avoid the sports section because sports fans watch sports rather than participate in them.

In many metropolitan areas, school owners have a variety of newspapers to choose from and should focus on ones with a local readership. In the future, newspapers may attract a larger online readership. Until then, avoid buying an advertising package that includes online and hard-copy advertisements until you have a strong feel for your market and have developed a track record of successful advertising.

Magazine Advertising

Why should a martial arts business owner want to advertise in a magazine? There are three main reasons.

First, an ad in a large publication like *Black Belt, Inside Kung Fu* or *Taekwondo Times* can be used to establish credibility in other advertising mediums. For example, if you publish an item in *Black Belt,* you can then say in your local advertisements: "as seen in *Black Belt* magazine." Members of the AIKIA organization have used this approach by pooling their resources. While a full-page ad could cost $1,500, having 50 people participate makes it much more affordable. Once you place your ad, you can refer back to the same insertion in a popular martial arts publication for years.

Magazine advertising can also bring in revenue from tourism. If your school is located in an area that attracts tourists, a local vacation-oriented magazine ad can provide exposure to anyone visiting the area. It could be that your club sells T-shirts or other gear that people will purchase as souvenirs. Combining a popular tourist attraction name or city with the words karate, taekwondo or mixed martial arts could prove to be a moneymaker.

A third reason to advertise in a magazine is simply to sell merchandise. The martial arts entrepreneur who came up with the MMA conditioning program has made a mint. He sells the program through *Black Belt.* Many talented martial artists have sold videos and other specialty items through magazines. If you have the skill and personality and can transfer that charisma to video, consider developing a video program and advertising.

To get started, call ad reps from the magazines. Most have toll-free phone numbers, so call them and ask for a media kit. In most cases, you will have to send them the ad. The magazine staff can produce an ad for you, but it is costly. Unless you are confident that you will recoup the costs or your school is so large that you can easily absorb the loss, magazine advertising may not prove to be cost-effective.

Placing the same quarter-page ad on pages that face each other is one of the most successful ad tactics I use to promote the Karate College summer camp. On the next page, the duplicate ads catch people's attention, and most readers will take the time to compare the ads to ensure that they match. The result: People are far more likely to read the duplicate ads than a standard one.

viduals and companies to trade with one another in an online marketplace, as a way to attract business to their Web sites. If you try one of these outlets, consider offering a "cost leader." Cost leaders are low-cost incentives, like below-market prices for gloves, gi, hand wraps, etc., to encourage readers to visit your Web site. There are a multitude of opportunities on the Internet, but remember to pay attention to your market. Only target the directories that your potential customers may read. Also, be aware of potential Internet scams involving copycat Craigslist and eBay businesses.

A few years ago, most school owners would compete for the largest ads in traditional phone directories like the Yellow Pages. Because people can now track down business information on their cell phones or computers, the effectiveness of a Yellow Pages ad has diminished considerably.

Today, fewer school owners advertise through the Yellow Pages. If you plan to use traditional directories, consider a small color ad with an image. List your phone number, school address, e-mail address and a few catch phrases like "family friendly" and "money back guaranteed." "Free offer," "certified," "safe" and "reliable" are also always effective.

Many directory ads fail because they're designed to boost their owner's egos rather than attract customers. Because so many ads promote their school's instructor as either a 10th dan or national champion, readers quickly become unresponsive to such claims.

To make the most of your investment, use your directory space to get prospects to visit your Web site. Consider posting on Craigslist (www.craigslist.org), which hosts local classified sections for more than 550 cities. Some school owners also regularly offer merchandise on eBay (www.ebay.com), which allows indi-

attract business to their Web sites. If you try one of these outlets, consider offering a "cost leader." Cost leaders are low-cost incentives, like below-market prices for gloves, gi, hand wraps, etc., to encourage readers to visit your Web site. There are a multitude A few years ago, most school owners would compete for the largest ads in traditional phone directories like the Yellow Pages. Because people can now track down business information on their cell phones or computers, the effectiveness of a Yellow Pages ad has diminished considerably.

Today, fewer school owners advertise through the Yellow Pages. If you plan to use traditional directories, consider a small color ad with an image. List your phone number, school address, e-mail address and a few catch phrases like "family friendly" and "money back guaranteed." "Free offer," "certified," "safe" and "reliable" are also always effective.

Many directory ads fail because they're designed to boost their owner's egos rather than attract customers. Because so many ads promote their school's instructor as either a 10th dan or national champion, readers quickly become unresponsive to such claims.

To make the most of your investment, use your directory space to get prospects to visit your Web site. Consider posting on Craigslist (www.craigslist.org), which hosts local classified sections for more than 550 cities. Some school owners also regularly offer merchandise on eBay (www.ebay.com), which allows individuals and companies to trade with one another in an online marketplace, as a way to

be aware of potential Internet scams involving copycat Craigslist and eBay businesses.

A few years ago, most school owners would compete for the largest ads in traditional phone directories like the Yellow Pages. Because people can now track down business information on their cell phones or computers, the effectiveness of a Yellow Pages ad has diminished considerably.

Today, fewer school owners advertise through the Yellow Pages. If you plan to use traditional directories, consider a small color ad with an image. List your phone number, school address, e-mail address and a few catch phrases like "family friendly" and "money back guaranteed." "Free offer," "certified," "safe" and "reliable" are also always effective.

Many directory ads fail because they're designed to boost their owner's egos rather than attract customers. Because so many ads promote their school's instructor as either a

Yellow Pages Ads/Internet Listings

A few years ago, most school owners would compete for the largest ads in traditional phone directories like the Yellow Pages. Because people can now track down business information on their cell phones or computers, the effectiveness of a Yellow Pages ad has diminished considerably.

Today, fewer school owners advertise through the Yellow Pages. If you plan to use traditional directories, consider a small color ad with an image. List your phone number, school address, e-mail address and a few catch phrases like "family friendly" and "money back guaranteed." "Free offer," "certified," "safe" and "reliable" are also always effective.

Many directory ads fail because they're designed to boost their owner's egos rather than attract customers. Because so many ads promote their school's instructor as either a 10th dan or national champion, readers quickly become unresponsive to such claims.

To make the most of your investment, use your directory space to get prospects to visit your Web site. Consider posting on Craigslist (www.craigslist.org), which hosts local classified sections for more than 550 cities. Some school owners also regularly offer merchandise on eBay (www.ebay.com), which allows individuals and companies to trade with one another in an online marketplace, as a way to attract business to their Web sites. If you try one of these outlets, consider offering a "cost leader." Cost leaders are low-cost incentives, like below-market prices for gloves, gi, hand wraps, etc., to encourage readers to visit your Web site. There are a multitude of opportunities on the Internet, but remember to pay attention to your market. Only target the directories that your potential customers may read. Also, be aware of potential Internet scams involving copycat Craigslist and eBay businesses.

Radio Advertising

Martial arts school owners seldom use radio advertising. You have to match the right message to the right station and be heard at the right time by your specific target audience, which is not an easy task.

Several years ago, I developed an effective radio ad. My spokesman—who used a Chinese dialect similar to the one found in the TV series *Kung Fu*—announced the grand opening of my new school while the song "Everybody Was Kung Fu Fighting" played in the background. The ad ran on a radio station that teenagers listened to while getting ready for school. Scores of people told me that they heard the ad on the radio. It was a great way to create an immediate buzz about a new karate school. I combined the radio ad with press releases, a demonstration at the local mall and a display ad in the newspaper.

Radio advertising is most useful when you have a big event, such as a grand opening or a celebrity appearance, and you combine it with other forms of advertising to get your message out to the public. Short 15- to 30-second spots repeated two to three times during the space of one hour tend to work best.

Other radio ideas include going on the air to discuss a charity event that you are sponsoring or asking a local radio announcer to repeatedly promote your school during the show. Commit to one, maybe two, stations, but if you receive no response from the public, then mark radio advertising off your "to-do" list.

TV Advertising

While cable and satellite TV advertising is effective, it's often too expensive. If you have a contact at a local TV station, ask your contact for the details on posting an ad, but proceed with caution because production charges often are cost-prohibitive.

A rule of thumb: If you can identify a show and a time that you think most of your target audience is watching, then proceed. As with radio, TV advertising is useful for big events, but it is too costly for everyday advertising. Remember, you must match the message, time and station to be successful in reaching your target audience.

Many areas have public-access television. If you have the talent, looks and personality to become a TV personality, contact the station. You could get lucky and find a station manager who likes martial arts and will air your concept. Programs that feature martial arts might include martial arts fitness, self-defense or the history and culture of a particular art. Consider recording a concept program yourself. Play it to students. Take it to public schools or find other appropriate audiences. The reaction of your audience will let you know whether your concept has potential.

Billboard Advertising

You seldom see billboards dedicated to martial arts schools because renting them is expensive. Still, it is worthwhile to contact a billboard ad provider. Sometimes a sign is not in use, and you can get it for less than half price.

Design your billboard ad like any print ad, but be brief and get to the point. Include a logo or image that will attract attention. Drivers only have seconds to read your message, so a school name, phone number or an easy-to-remember Web site might be all the information you can display effectively. If the billboard is not lit at night, then your ad is of no use during those hours.

When I first opened a school, I asked for and received permission from a landowner to erect a large, billboard-type sign. The sign was 6 feet by 8 feet. I had to apply to the state commission, and I was granted a one year lease. The cost for the state lease was reasonable, and the cost to build the sign was only a few hundred dollars. My sign simply displayed the name of my school with the phone number underneath.

Because everyone who entered or exited the town used the same highway, I found the billboard ad to be my single most effective use of advertising dollars. Billboard advertisements gave me the additional benefit of having a perceived location without extra costs. If you can make the right deal, billboard space might work for you.

Web Sites

Web sites have become essential information and advertising spaces for martial arts school owners. If you lack the design and technical skills, it's likely that one of your students has the ability to make and post a Web site. Often, you can co-op with other businesses that rent or sell Internet domains. This same cooperative approach is used when a number of schools get together to purchase advertising space in a magazine.

The purpose of school Web sites vary, as do the results. Typically, you want to list class times, give a few testimonials, and describe your background, program and facilities. Be concise and to the point.

Because Web sites offer more space than brochures, the information you place on your site can be more comprehensive. It is also available 24 hours a day, and Web sites are both easier and cheaper to edit than print ads.

Web site creation is limited only by your imagination and creativity. To have an effective site, you do not have to possess a full understanding of Web design. Instead, you need to know how to promote your services effectively and present a professional image to your site.

First, you need to acquire the services of a Web-hosting company. Web hosts are companies that provide Web space, domain names and an Internet connection. Companies such as Freeservers.com and Godaddy.com offer different pricing packages depending on what services you desire. There are even options for free Web hosting; however, it is recommended that you avoid the free hosting packages if possible because the hosting company receives money for posting other companies' ads on your site. Sign up for a fee-based service and control everything on your site. Typically, the cheapest option usually provides the necessary services to operate your site.

You will most likely use your hosting company to pick out and register your domain name, which is the name and location of your school on the Internet. For example, Blackbeltmag.com is *Black Belt* magazine's domain name. Take your time and research the available domain names for your school before settling on one. Because of the size of the Internet, most single words and abbreviations are already used, so pick a full name or phrase to identify your school. This will be the link to your school, so you will want it to be something that people can remember and associate with your school. It is your Web site's identity.

You have several options for creating the pages for your site. One option is to have someone else construct the pages. Find a student who can put together the site, or hire a professional Web designer to create a site.

If you choose to do it yourself, either use a Web-design program or the site-creation tools provided by your hosting company. Both options will allow you to concentrate on the content of your pages without having to learn a lot of HTML, which is the programming language used by many Web sites. Web-design programs such as Dreamweaver or FrontPage allow you to create Web pages by dropping pictures and text wherever you want them. Most hosting companies provide templates that you can place text or pictures into.

A lot of effort should be put into the design and content of your site so it's information rich and easy to navigate. In creating my own site, I received assistance from one of my students, John Miller, who designed both www.aikia.net and his own Web site www.kyuusai.org. Here is a short list of guidelines for creating your site:

Make the content as useful as possible.

Keep your audience in mind, and post information that current and prospective students will be looking for, including your background, class schedule, facilities and a description of your program.

Keep the information lean and clean.

Do not include too many topics on one page, and try to limit the information on the page. Be descriptive and specific.

Update pages often so people return to the site frequently.

Include news and events, such as seminar and testing dates.

Give your pages a consistent and user-friendly appearance.

Make your page easier to read by using basic color schemes and font types, have navigation menus on the top and bottom of each page, and maintain a consistent layout from page to page.

Design the site to be search-engine friendly. A search engine, such as Google.com, is a dedicated Web site used to find things on the Internet. Every Web site will have a source code. The search engine uses keywords and other information to categorize your Web site and make it easier for a person to find. A popular strategy for optimizing your search-engine results is inserting keywords in a meta tag (embedded in the source code). Even though your site may be listed as "karate," you will want to add words like taekwondo, kung fu and *jiu-jitsu* in the meta tag. (You can even use phrases like Mr. Miyagi, mixed-martial arts or Bruce Lee.) By adding the keywords in your meta tag, you increase the possibility that the search engine will identify your page with the keywords someone searches for. You may also want to add your site to a paid advertising program known as "sponsored sites," which will locate sponsored sites in a separate section to the right of each Google.com search. Here are some techniques that you can use to improve how your site ranks on major search-engine sites:

Learn by example.

Do a search to see how the top sites phrase things. What are the keywords on their site? What are they doing to get ranked so high? Answer these questions and implement some of the same strategies.

Make friends.

Get other relevant sites to set up links to your site, especially those that rank higher than yours.

Use static text links to make it easier for search engines to navigate your site.

Avoid using image links, java navigation menus, frames and image maps. Search engines use automated software (called spiders or crawlers) to look at your Web site. This software works best with static text links and cannot read or follow the links and pages used by text alternatives.

Use keywords that you want people to use to find your site.

Use these keywords as much as possible, especially in the page's title and the first paragraph. The keywords are the basic information displayed in most search-engine results. Make sure the keywords are integrated smoothly within the page's content.

Be descriptive and accurate.

The largest and most popular search engines typically ignore HTML code that lists keywords and random text on the page. The search sites do not want to rely on what people say their site contains; they search the content of the site and determine what the keywords are for themselves.

Once your site is up, actively work to promote it. The more people visit your site, the more effective it will be. Below is an example of a successful Web site.

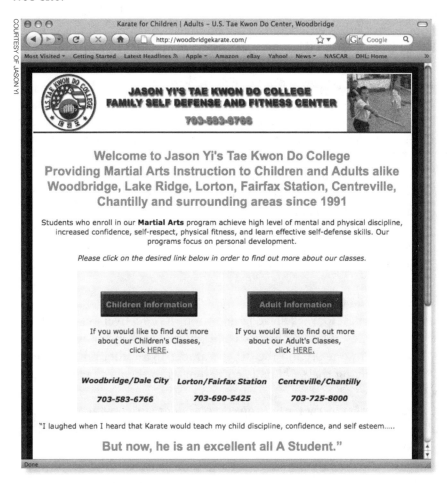

Word-of-Mouth Advertising

One of the most effective forms of advertising, when used in conjunction with all the other forms discussed in this chapter, is word of mouth, and it begins at your school. Talk to your members. Listen to their questions. Develop "affirmations." A friend of mine used to open every class with a question. He would yell, "Class, how do you feel?" The class would respond, "Happy, healthy and terrific, sir!"

Another example of an affirmation is what my mentor used to greet a player or guest. He would say, "What a day!" And the player would respond, "What a day, coach!" The meaning was simple: "What a day to do my best!"

When every student feels that every class is "What a class!" or that members are "happy, healthy and terrific," they will enthusiastically tell their peers about your school. While examining internal promotions in the next few chapters, I will revisit the importance of word-of-mouth advertising.

How Do I Know Whether My Ad Is Working?

In your ad, do you make the reader an offer? Is your heading clear and easy to understand? Is your ad copy edited for mistakes? Is your contact information clear and easy to find? Finally, are you answering the question that all prospects have: "What's in it for me?"

Show your ads to your students, their parents and the ad rep you're working with. Ask them for their opinion. Provide several choices and then go with the most popular.

Are you tracking your ads? Ask each caller or prospect who contacts you, "How did you hear about us?" Take notes. An ad is quite an investment, so if it works, great. Use the ad repeatedly. Otherwise, try something new.

Track Your Ads and Create Urgency

It is important to track an ad to determine its effectiveness. If you have two phone lines at your school—a cell-phone number will work—place one number in one ad and the other number in another ad. The phone number receiving the most calls corresponds to the ad that solicits the best response.

Your ad must attract attention. If you're not sure how to do that, the ad rep from the company that you're working with will be acquainted with ad components such as borders, headlines, photos and other illustrations. By creating a sense of urgency, you most likely will get an immediate and direct response from the ad. Remember to find a good graphic artist to work with you if you plan to create your own ads. Most colleges, trade schools and some high schools will have an abundance of talented graphic artists if you need low-cost assistance.

An effective short-term ad may include a closing date for a free offer or have a clip-out coupon with the statement: "Offer valid through (date)." This type of ad is said to have a "call to action." If the reader wants to take advantage of the free offer, then that person must take action now.

Avoid Mistakes

I want to mention one last thing: Although I have covered the best ways to advertise, you will have many opportunities and options for advertising. When I first started, someone told me to get the message out any way I could. Bad idea. I once paid several hundred dollars to put my school name on the back of a permanent bench in a bowling center. The salesperson told me that every person who came to bowl would see my ad. I was impressed. The logic was flawed, though, because bowlers already have a hobby: bowling. When you spend your advertising dollars, be cautious.

Advertising, when properly carried out, will get prospective students to visit your school. Do not try to sell a program to them in the ad or on the phone when they call. Your goal is to get them to participate in a free class.

CHAPTER 6

PUBLIC RELATIONS

PUBLIC RELATIONS

*public opinion • your image • PR moments • demos
media releases • other types of public relations • example campaign*

Publicity is much more than just free advertising. It's also about increasing the public's awareness of your business, which can become the single most effective way to bring students to your school. This is great when the publicity is good, but it can hurt your business when the publicity is unfavorable.

Whenever you interact with the public, you have the opportunity to create, develop or change your image. To shape your image effectively, you must discover and evaluate how the public perceives you and your school. Generating publicity is only one part of the equation. Making sure that the publicity is favorable is the other.

For example, you may choose to promote your achievement in martial arts using the PR methods that I will outline in this chapter. If you have a special rank or training under a well-known master instructor, then promote that achievement. If you have earned college degrees, then use that education to your advantage. These accomplishments help you build credibility.

Like advertising, public relations is a continuous process that requires a lot of effort, but the results are usually worth it. Using easy-to-apply methods, you can create and reinforce the image you want to convey to the public, so take action to gain control over how the public perceives you.

How to Get the Public's Opinion

One way to find out how the public perceives you and your school is to conduct a survey. Also, listen to what members, parents and visitors have to say about your club.

Even though you might receive some negative comments, place a box in your office and invite members to write comments and suggestions. Ask the students what you are doing right.

The next time you have a demonstration, have a few parents or friends ask attendees what they think of your school. Solicit information about how the audience liked the demonstration. What did people like best? Was there anything that they didn't like?

You don't always need to ask for advice to find out what the public thinks. Along with listening to people, keep track of what's popular to determine what strategies are working. Is a piece of equipment being used more frequently? Is a particular class being taken more than other classes?

By finding out the public's opinion, you'll be able to develop or improve your eventual PR campaign, which will include four features:

Education

It is your responsibility to educate your potential market about the positive benefits of training at your school. Accept all requests for speaking engagements. Use lectures and demonstrations to inspire your target market to become involved and inform the public about your club activities.

Motivation

Because many potential students fear getting hurt or embarrassed at a martial arts class, you must motivate the public to get involved. During your demonstrations or public speaking engagements, get audience members on their feet to participate in a free, informal class by creating attention-grabbing programs like "The Top 10 Self-Defense Techniques." Organize 10 popular self-defense escapes, such as how to escape from a bear hug or choke. Make sure each skill is user-friendly and perfectly safe.

Consideration

Do not be inconsiderate and critical of participants. Be an encourager, not a discourager, so that they will love your program. Remember, organize for and speak to the beginners in your audience. Advanced students, black belts and competitors already have their own opinions about your style or school. A public demonstration or seminar is not the preferred time to try to change their opinions. I bring this up because I have seen many instructors design their programs to impress their competitors instead of their target market. When you focus on your competitors' talking points, you run the risk of missing your own specific market and your own unique message. Speak to the beginners. They are your potential students.

Recognition

Regularly inform the public of new developments at your school. If a child wins a trophy, if you give a speaking engagement or if you have a notable visitor drop by your club, inform them.

Refuse to Be Negative

A popular saying that applies to negative comments is: "When you throw dirt, you give up ground." In order to build themselves up, some people believe that they must put others down. If you want your school to have a positive image, do not follow their example. Even when you're describing your competition, you should refuse to be negative.

While at times it's OK to listen to a complaint about a competitor, your response should be constructive and positive. Remember, a visitor who complains about the other school will most likely complain about you if given the opportunity. Defining your school with a positive attitude begins with the first introduction and can affect how prospects perceive your program.

Here are two examples of how negativity can ruin a performance and your image. I once hired a *ninjutsu* instructor to teach at a summer camp. Instead of teaching the high points of his system, he devoted his time to degrading other arts that opposed his system. When his class was over, he had managed to teach only one technique. The rest of the time had been wasted on negative remarks. He was not hired for the next camp.

I also witnessed a kickboxing instructor give into negativity at a shopping-center promotion. At the beginning of his demonstration, the instructor recognized two advanced students from a competitor's karate school. The kickboxing instructor immediately began to change his message from the health benefits of kickboxing to why the kata in karate was outdated and of little use. He lost his audience, who had come to hear about the benefits of kickboxing, and failed to attract new students.

So remember, giving into negativity can doom any public performance, private discussion or positive image.

Building Your Professional Image

Creating a positive public image and improving your credibility is also a continous process. Here are 10 steps that should be considered when building your professional image:

1. Make an effort to gain certifications.

Use everything from college degrees to seminar certificates to build credibility. Each time you receive a certificate or membership, consider sending a press release to your local media. Discuss the importance of the certification in your monthly newsletter.

2. Become a resident authority.

Be perceived by the public as an authority or a "local expert." Accept speaking engagements. Be willing to be interviewed. When your public thinks martial arts, they should think of you.

3. Write, publish and create.

Write your own e-book about martial arts. Use articles, magazines and fliers to let the public know about you and your club. People will believe what they see.

4. Speak.

Get out and be seen. Develop an image so people will get to know you. Volunteer to do speeches at conferences and charity events. Be available for demos at local festivals and other events.

5. Become an adviser.

Get involved and develop an advisory board for your club or become an adviser for someone else. One way to do this is to become an adviser for a local recreation program like the YMCA.

6. Link your school to a celebrity or charity.

Donate time and money to a charity. Offer to collect money through board breaking or kicking marathons. Show an interest in community service.

7. Carry business cards or buttons with you.

When you meet and greet people, give them a card or button. Doing so allows them to associate something with your martial arts school.

8. Look and act the part.

Get in shape. Dress properly. Present a good appearance and healthy lifestyle.

9. Develop a media kit.

A media kit contains information about your club. It includes photos, biographies, member lists, program descriptions and testimonials.

Use the media kit when promoting public relations with newspaper, radio and TV requests.

10. Sponsor a team.

Donate T-shirts with your name and logo to a winning softball or basketball team. Often, you will be permitted to perform a demo at a game.

The Importance of the Demo Team

One of the best publicity tools you have is your demo team. A demo team that captivates its audience will attract new students to your school and generate word-of-mouth advertising, so take control of your publicity campaign by shaping an exciting and informative team. Students love to participate in demonstrations, and parents love to see their kids perform. Create opportunities for your team and take them on the road.

It is also important that you match your demonstrations with the public's interest. For example, if self-defense for kids is an important public issue and if you are an expert in that field, then by all means let the public know that you are available. Let's suppose that a new martial arts flick with a positive message like *The Karate Kid* (1984) or *Kung Fu Panda* (2008) is opening at a local movie theater. If you can convince the theater that your demonstration complements the movie, your team will have the opportunity to perform at the introduction of the movie. Before the demonstration, contact local media outlets; you might end up with free TV and newspaper coverage. We call these opportunities "PR moments," and it's up to you to identify and create them.

There are three popular formats for demonstrations aimed at educating the public and motivating prospective students to join your school. They include the movie-premiere demo, the mall demo and the physical-education class demo. In each case, you must make sure that you give your demo team sufficient rehearsal and preparation time. Also, determine a set number of new network and recruitment contacts that you want to achieve. Don't forget that your demo must target and address a specific audience, market or demographic.

The Movie-Premiere Demo

The premiere of a new movie featuring martial arts in a positive light is almost always going to represent a perfect PR moment for gaining positive publicity for your school, seminar or training camp. Here are some ways to gain publicity for your school by identifying your program with a successful movie campaign:

Plan your publicity campaign at least one month in advance of the premiere at your local theater.

If you have competitors in your immediate area, you might need more time to secure exclusivity. Contact the theater owner or a regional distributor to gain access to the movie premiere.

Organize your demo around the theme of the movie.

For *The Karate Kid*, sending a traditional white gi-clad team would have been appropriate. For *Kung Fu Panda*, mentioning animals associated with kung fu would be a good selection. Use your professional instincts to play to the crowd.

Send a press release to the entertainment editor of the local newspaper.

Make sure you include details about the movie and how your demo will add to the movie premiere.

Ask whether you can set up a small martial arts display one week before to attract more attention to your demo.

Movie-theater owners are in the business of selling tickets. They won't mind helping you promote your business if in turn they see greater ticket sales.

If possible, set up a lead-box display.

Use a lead box to display images of your school and familiarize the public with your programs. This also helps you generate "leads" for prospects interested in your programs.

Ask to begin your demo a few hours before the movie begins.

You can also continue demos for as long as the movie runs that day.

Work the crowd. Have business cards and fliers ready.

Designate a "lead" person or yourself to work the audience. Give away offers of up to 30 days of free instruction at your school.

The lead person should distribute cards, answer questions, ask questions and collect information such as names, addresses, phone numbers and e-mails when possible.

Play dynamic music and have the team members *kiai* loudly at every opportunity.

The music and kiai will attract attention and increase the size of your audience.

At the end of the day, thank your leaders and reward your team members.

Everyone appreciates a pat on the back. Be genuine and generous with your compliments.

Follow up on every prospective lead.

Call to encourage potential clients to attend the first free class.

Remember, the movie-premiere demo can be an effective opportunity to promote your image, meet and greet the public, and publicize your school. After you have organized and participated in a few movie premieres, your demo team should be prepared for each new opportunity. Some members will naturally serve as primary performers, while others will be greeters. Learn to work together as a unit so that every performer has an equally valuable role. At the completion of each demo, praise each participant for a job well done.

The Mall Demo

It is important that you maximize the potential for each and every PR moment.

The movie premiere presents an excellent one, but find other PR moments that are right for your business. If you have a local mall or shopping center, enlist your demo team to present a program there. Generally, offer to demonstrate for any business that will extend the invitation.

If you discover that a new business will open soon, contact the business representative and offer to present a demo during the opening-day ceremony. An important component in developing a PR campaign is to earn the public's acceptance. When you achieve a positive public image in which the public demonstrates a need for your expertise, you will be rewarded with public acceptance. In other words, you will achieve public acceptance as the expert in your field or business. With each demonstration you give, you increase the likelihood that the public will identify your school as the first choice for martial arts instruction in your community.

Set up and organize the mall demo just like you would organize the movie premiere demo. Follow each step.

The Physical-Education Class Demo

While the movie premiere typically happens only once or twice a year and mall demos should be set no more than once a quarter, you can hold a physical-education class demo on a weekly basis. Public educators are always looking for ways to get their students excited about learning.

Using these key points to promote your demo, public-school principals will most likely accept you and your program or direct you to the right person to contact. If you know the name of a particular teacher, consider contacting that teacher directly. Offer to teach a class for him or her. In some cases, like a physical-education class, you might get the invitation to teach for the entire day.

Again, remember to mention key components of your lecture or demonstration while speaking to an educator. These components show that your demo is extremely relevant to the students. The following are the most effective key components:

Fitness

You will teach students about specific fitness methods related to martial arts training.

Cultural Diversity

You will present a demo that examines the societies that shaped the Asian arts.

Self-Defense

You will encourage each student to participate in simple, easy-to-perform techniques that teach effective self-defense tactics.

Many instructors try to win over public-school educators by focusing primarily on self-defense. If you include cultural diversity and fitness in your pitch, you will find greater acceptance for your program and demo.

The Press

The press release, also known as the news release or media release, is another effective way to update the public about your club. A press release is a faux news story that provides media outlets with enough information to cover whatever event or accomplishment you are promoting. Like most news stories, a press release should be written in third person, relevant to the readers of the publication and include quotes from people who were involved in the story such as from yourself or from your students. Because you want your school to be covered positively, the tone and content of your release should reflect that. Never be negative.

To increase the chances of your story getting covered, send the press release to the editors and producers who are in charge of covering that topic. If the story's about a competition, send it to the sports editor. If it's entertainment related, such as a movie-premiere demo, send it to the lifestyle or entertainment editor. Sometimes, it won't be immediately obvious who to send the press release to. For example, if the release is promoting a new program for a local church group, ask someone at the media outlet who to send it to.

Before writing your release, call or visit the media outlet and ask the editors what they look for in a press release. The editor will probably tell you that the release must be newsworthy. To determine whether their publication will use a press release, editors usually consider the following:

Is it extraordinary?

Is it a story about how you broke 10 bricks, or how you completed 100 sit-ups in one minute? Maybe you are celebrating your 20th year as a business in your community. That is extraordinary.

Is your news/information unusual?

Perhaps all 10 of your students placed high at a tournament. Maybe you met Chuck Norris or another champion at an event. If you go out of state to complete a course of instruction under a world champion or master, you should write a press release and have it published.

Does your news/information have universal or immediate appeal?

Can all readers relate to your success? Maybe members of your aerobic kickboxing class lost a combined 1,000 pounds. Newspaper readers would be interested in how they did it. Most readers can relate to the topic of weight loss.

Use the press release to generate publicity and to inform others of up-coming events and performances inside and outside your school. Be creative and timely with your press release. For example, if you have a rank exam or demo, don't wait until the week of the event to send out the release. If anything, send it out at least two to three weeks before. Or it may be better to call the media outlet to see when they like to be informed.

Seven Steps to Writing a Winning Press Release

When writing your press releases, address the following seven steps:

1. Who?

Be brief but precise when describing the topic you want covered.

2. What?

What exactly took place? In the case of the aerobic kickboxing class, the 20 students who were enrolled lost a combined 1,000 pounds.

3. When?

Use specific dates and time frames.

4. Where?

Be specific when providing your location, and consider including directions or a landmark. Also, make sure the information is easy to spot on the release.

5. Why?

Describe the reason for the event or performance.

6. How?

How did it happen? What caused the weight loss? Was it a new program? Did the students sign a pact in which each one agreed to lose a specific number of pounds?

7. Edit your release.

Be sure to check your facts, and proofread for spelling and grammatical errors. Editors receive a lot of press releases every day, so make sure yours looks prefessional.

Here's a mock-up press release that a martial arts school owner may write about weight loss.

For Immediate Release

Fitness Kickboxing Group Sheds 1,000 Pounds!

Glenvar, VA (November 20, 2008)—Twenty members of the Well's Fitness Kickboxing class lost a combined 1,000 pounds with the help of instructor Mike Wells. The class began the one-year program on January 10, 2007.

After group leader Martha Mays examined the charts, she noted that the group's total weight loss was 1,000 pounds as of January 10, 2008, exactly one year from the day the class was formed. "We each signed a pact not to cheat on our calorie intake outside of class," Mays said. "This was the hardest-working class I have ever had," Wells added. "We instituted a new program this year, and the results are incredible."

Members lost an average of 29 pounds each, with one member dropping an incredible 76 pounds. "The weight-loss program combines a fun and vigorous kickboxing routine with individual nutritional programs," Wells said. "But what makes the program unique is that each member signs a pact to encourage each other," Mays added. "We have daily e-mail reminders. We phone each other weekly. We've become like family."

For more information about the fitness kickboxing program, contact Wells or Mays at 555-1212 or visit their Web site at www.glenvarkickboxfit.org.

In the example, the number "1,000" made the story "extraordinary." Any group that loses 1,000 pounds combined will tend to win reader interest and approval. Because the story has universal appeal, a newspaper editor will probably want to expand it into a feature story. To increase the chances of getting the story printed, the press release should also include high-quality "before" and "after" photos. It adds visual interest to the story and shows editors that the extraordinary event is credible.

Include a Photo

You have heard the expression, "A picture is worth a thousand words." In print media, it's true. Sometimes the photo will sell the press release or article even if there is no universal appeal. By including a high-quality image of a unique subject, you improve your chances of getting your press release release published.

Sources for Press Releases

When you send your press release to the local newspaper and to radio or TV stations, be sure to address the release to a person. Call the station and tell the receptionist that you need a name and address for the entertainment editor. If you have a copy of the newspaper, you can usually find the name and e-mail address of the appropriate person near the byline or at the end of the story.

When you call, say that you are sending a press release. Ask for the name, e-mail address and job title of the person who should receive the release. Also ask whether the media outlet has special requirements for releases. Media outlets need newsworthy stories and inspiring photos. Even if the people in charge choose not to use your release, they will be pleased to review it. Getting two to three stories published each year should be your goal.

After the editor runs your first press release as a story, take a few minutes to stop by the office and thank him or her. Mention a story by the editor that you read and liked. Get to know the people who can help your business grow.

Business Cards

Business cards serve the dual purpose of advertisement and public relations. You can hand out the cards at PR events or you can post the cards at local businesses as an inexpensive form of advertising. Cards are cost-effective and should be handed out on all occasions. Here are some ideas to help make your business-card campaign successful:

Develop a school logo or design, and include it on the card.

An attractive logo can make your identity unique. You can use the logo for T-shirts, fliers, business cards and other items to promote your school.

Include your name, phone number, location and e-mail/Web site address.

Be sure that the information you provide makes it easy to locate your school. Most card companies have a set price for up to four lines. You can add more lines or even change the color of your type, but it will increase your price.

Discuss your goals for the card with your printer and school members before making a final decision.

Take a copy of the final design to your school and ask members for their feedback.

Make your cards effective and easy to use with a standard size.

Opting for an odd-size card adds to your cost of production. The double card, which is folded, works no better than the single card with printing on both sides.

Do research.

Before you decide on a design, look around and compare your concept with other cards.

Some instructors prefer to put a free offer on the back of their business cards, such as, "Turn in this card for a 30-day free trial." Other instructors print a map on the back to help prospective clients locate the studio. Regardless of the design, most instructors distribute the cards on bulletin boards and other places of business throughout the community.

If you have a group of enthusiastic members, encourage them to distribute the cards to their friends and acquaintances.

Fliers

When I operated a taekwondo school in a small college town, fliers were my main source of advertising and publicity. Because my school was located one block from the main college campus, most of my students were from the college. As a result, I could hang the fliers on the posting boards of dorms and academic buildings. Each week, members of my school were assigned buildings where they would display fliers.

An effective flier, like the one below, follows these guidelines:

76

Design an attractive flier with a strong border.

Chances are your flier will be placed next to others, and an attractive border or design will help it stand out.

Make your contact information easy to find.

Consider placing your phone number or Web address on several strips at the bottom of the page. Interested readers may pull off info strips instead of writing down the information themselves.

Use a great photo.

A flier with an image will attract far more attention than a flier with no picture. Action shots seem to work best. The most talked-about photo I used featured me with Chuck Norris back in the 1970s. A celebrity image will attract attention. If you're selling fitness, include an image of a super-fit man or woman. To advertise your kids program, include photos of kids enjoying the class.

Use the standard full page of 8-1/2 inches by 11 inches.

This size is cost-effective and readily available.

Be brief with your message.

Most often a photo or attractive image with a few lines of basic information works best. If you have more messages than you can put on one flier, post multiple fliers with different messages.

Post your flier on message boards in your community.

Do not randomly put up fliers without permission because they will be discarded. Refrain from putting fliers on parked car windows because they tend to annoy prospects. Ever come back to your car and see a piece of paper on the windshield? You assume it's a parking ticket and your defenses go up. Find boards that are often used, ensuring that your flier will be noticed in a positive way.

Use fliers to announce belt testing, seminars and class schedules.

Fliers can be used to recognize members who have won tournaments, belt ranks, etc. You can also identify testing dates and free classes or clinics to entice readers to visit your school.

Remember that fliers are used to announce current events and programs. They are among the most useful and low-cost advertising/publicity aids available.

The door hanger is another option that serves a similar purpose as the flier. A door hanger is an oblong piece of paper that is cut so that one end of the paper fits around a doorknob. You have no doubt encountered door hangers promoting pizza deliveries, political candidates and yard work. Use the door hanger to provide publicity for important events at your school. Have several students walk through selected neighborhoods and place door hangers on front doors. The best time to place them is in the afternoon before residents return home from work. Because some residents may not be fond of door hangers, limit your door-hanging activities to one or two times a year per neighborhood. Be advised that the door-hanger campaign can be very time-consuming.

Newsletters

The newsletter can be a one- to two-page (or more) document with brief news stories and photos. It is an effective PR tool that can be distributed to every member, former member and interested party on your list. You can use your newsletter to place advertisements and build member loyalty. Expensive hard-copy newsletters have been replaced with low-cost e-mail newsletters. Some ideas for a newsletter are as follows:

ILLUSTRATIONS COURTESY OF NAPMA

Begin your newsletter with a testimonial or a quote from a club member.

Members typically enjoy the attention of being featured in the school newsletter. By using members in the newsletter, you will build readership.

Include as many photos as is practical for each newsletter.

Photos of members are always of interest. Consider placing the photo of each new member in a "Get Acquainted" section.

Include as many member names as possible in each newsletter.

Identify each student earning a new rank. Include the name of each person assisting with school activities. Try including a "parent of the month." Include a section for "best attendance records." It's easy to come up with ways to say nice things about members of your school.

Change topics with each newsletter.

Focus each newsletter on a particular topic, such as weight loss, rank testing, organizational news and personal interests. Because you change the topics, readers will be more interested to read the newsletter.

Include some research information when appropriate to provide expert advice on topics like weight loss or muscle soreness.

You can use a quote or two from a well-known expert. Or include calorie counts or low-calorie recipes. Members that want to loose weight appreciate the calorie guides. Your newsletter should high-light your students' accomplishments and the school's contributions to the community.

Once you begin a newsletter, continue circulating it until you close your school. If developing the newsletter consumes too much time, ask a trusted and loyal student to take over the responsibility while you become the consultant and proofreader. Don't allow anyone to send out your school newsletter without proofing every line.

Many computer programs have style guides that construct electronic newsletters. Make the newsletter informative and attractive, and keep it coming on a monthly basis.

Brochures

A quality brochure can create an image, educate, advertise and sell your services or products. The brochure is typically constructed using a single piece of paper arranged in three columns on the front and back containing a message that prospects want to read. The brochure is used primarily to prepare people for their first visit to your school.

Include in your brochere information about the instructor, style, school location and hours of operation. You can also include specific information to boost your credibility, promote your school's prestige, and highlight the services your school provides to the community. You may want to include answers to a "most often asked questions" section.

Here are six steps and the text of a brochure designed by the AIKIA martial arts organization, which is used in part by more than 1,000 schools. Adapt what you like and change the text to fit your specific needs. You can use the same text for your Web-page brochure.

1. Write a note of welcome.

Welcome to AIKIA. The American Independent Karate Instructors Association is a network of martial arts clubs throughout the United States, Canada, Mexico and Europe. AIKIA members may take a free week of instruction at any licensed AIKIA school.

2. Provide your professional credentials.

Instructors teaching with AIKIA have been personally trained by (insert the head instructor's name).

3. Address the topics of physical fitness, self-defense and cultural diversity.

Research shows that martial arts students are interested in physical fitness and self-defense. The methods incorporated in AIKIA martial arts are informative, fun and safe. What's more, AIKIA martial arts can be learned and performed by virtually everyone. Classes are designed to meet individual needs. No one, regardless of age, education or physical talents, is left out. AIKIA martial arts utilizes state-of-the-art improvements that have been tested in competition and on the street. The AIKIA system is designed to provide instruction in the advanced principles of self-defense (speed enhancement, mobility, specificity of training, etc.) during the early months of instruction. The result is that more students are taught the principles of self-defense in the shortest possible time. In addition, the aerobic principle is incorporated to increase physical fitness during each workout. In essence, the AIKIA system stresses a combination of principles that have been thoroughly researched and designed to meet the needs of modern-day Americans.

4. Provide for a philosophy of self-esteem.

Just as important as the physical skills is the philosophy of self-esteem and goal setting, which is included in each martial arts session. In this manner, AIKIA not only trains the body but also trains the mind. After nine months of AIKIA training, most students report increased self-esteem as their coordination, fitness level and personal self-confidence are carefully nurtured.

The slogan in martial arts is "Nothing is impossible." AIKIA martial arts training has been successful in unleashing the "inner winner" to make us all more successful in whatever areas we pursue. Martial arts training is a study of character building and self-perfection. Through AIKIA instruction, students find greater self-confidence and success on the job, in sports and in social relationships because their training helps them take control.

Students also report new pride in a trim, fit appearance and new security in their ability to defend themselves. The parents of teens and children report that AIKIA training builds athletic ability and improves self-image because students see themselves as "winners." School bullies are defeated not by fighting but by having the confidence to tell others including friends, teachers and parents about a threatening individual. In addition, the comradeship experienced by AIKIA martial arts members provides students with a feeling of importance and self-worth that is unique to the martial arts. Each of these concepts has been thoroughly researched by a professional educator to insure your success.

5. Discuss earning belt promotions and setting goals.

Following the concept of goal setting, the AIKIA programs have been designed to help each student decide on a particular course of study. The orange-belt program is designed for students seeking an introduction to martial arts training. Attainment of the orange belt usually takes nine to 10 months. However, a student can take as much time as needed to earn an orange belt. The orange belt signifies skills in karate kicking, punching and blocking, with an understanding of several martial arts.

The green-belt program represents an intermediate level of skill (halfway through the black-belt program). Generally, a student can attain a green belt in 15 to 18 months. Again, the student can take as much time as needed without increasing the cost of the green-belt program. At the green-belt level, the student understands the philosophy of martial arts and can exhibit excellent skills in self-defense, form and movement.

By far, the most popular AIKIA course is the black-belt program. A black belt can be earned after 30 to 36 months of study. Attainment of a black belt is a supreme achievement, combining physical skills and mental power. Those who have attained a black belt have reported increased self-awareness, physical skill and self-confidence. The black belt need no loger fear or look up to anyone, for he or she has trained both mind and body to be beyond equal. Should his or her life be in danger—should there be a need to defend the rights of others—the true black belt may, without hesitation, go into action. The black belt no longer considers failure, for the training necessary to achieve a black belt has laid the ground-work for success. Regardless of your station in life, attainment of a black belt will prove a worthy and satisfying goal.

6. Include a final note about hidden values.

The national average for karate instruction by first- through third-degree black-belt instructors is $149 per month. AIKIA programs are priced significantly lower. As several business people have noted, AIKIA martial arts is obviously more concerned with making men and women than making money. Each program includes unlimited time and instruction. In other words, once you purchase an

AIKIA orange-, green- or black-belt program, you may take as much time as you require to reach your goal. There are no penalties or additional costs for taking more than the allotted time. What's more, you'll be setting your own goals on how best to pay off your own program. Most karate students begin a study of the martial arts in order to improve self-confidence, physical fitness, discipline, weight loss and ability in self-defense. AIKIA martial arts has continually proved successful in assisting each student to reach these goals. If AIKIA martial arts instruction can help you achieve your goals, then how much is it really worth? Certainly more than what you'll eventually pay per month! Think about it: If as a result of martial arts instruction you learn skills to improve your life, then can you measure such worth in dollars and cents? Isn't it time that you invest in yourself? The payoff could be more than you expect. Any of the AIKIA certified instructors can answer further questions and provide exact costs for each program. If you are not a class member, please call for an appointment. Call now! The first week is free.

The brochure provides introductory information and encourages prospective students to take a free class. The brochure also helps prepare the student for the costs associated with the program, which will be discussed in Chapter 8.

Give out brochures at every opportunity, such as at demos. Post your brochure on your Web site and ensure that it will be easy to download. Keep in mind that the brochure can be much more than a general description of your program.

DVD Brochure

Technological advances may eventually make the video brochure more cost-effective and better able to convey information than a printed brochure. If you have computer skills, you might be able to design and produce a DVD that acts as a brochure at a very low cost. Consider creating an introductory DVD for your school by having a student with video experience assist you.

Write a carefully designed script that follows the six steps discussed in the previous section, and keep it short: three to eight minutes max. Shoot the video, then record yourself or one of your students reading the script aloud to create a voice-over. Think of all your performers as actors playing a role in your brochure movie.

Display your video brochure on your Web site and upload it to YouTube (www.youtube.com), a free video-sharing site. You can also play a continuous loop of your video in the window of your studio. Distribute copies of your video to libraries and other locations that may be able to use it in a video display about martial arts.

Communitywide Publicity Campaign

An effective way to build a positive image for your school is to get involved with programs that promote public services. Typically, martial arts school owners become involved with programs like "stop the bully" or "stranger danger." Martial artists oftentimes also create programs that assist overweight kids with fitness goals. Most of these ideas, while admirable, are far too common to catch people's attention and fail to attract communitywide support. Sometimes you must think outside the box to come up with an attention-grabbing program that is in the public's interest and incorporates the specific martial arts lessons.

In 2002, I designed a program to address the topics of road rage and aggressive driving. By doing so, I avoided the obvious link to martial arts and self-defense. Instead, I highlighted the Asian martial arts' focus on courtesy because displays of courtesy and respect can help you resolve conflicts before they become violent. The following sections in this chapter will give you details on how to implement an in-depth communitywide public-interest publicity campaign.

My Road Rage Reducer Project was so successful that my research partner and I earned a highly competitive funding grant of $99,750 from the National Institutes of Health. I was interviewed on TV and radio shows across the country. Nationally, CNN News mentioned the project, and newspapers across the United States, Canada and Europe printed an Associated Press story about it.

The campaign to reduce road rage in my community covered a six-month period from October through March. Using government funding, I purchased advertising space on 17 billboards strategically located alongside every major highway used to enter or leave the town of Christiansburg, Virginia. Additional promotional materials included cards, fliers, a plug-in device called the "polite-lite" for drivers who can't use their hazard lights, and video programs demonstrating the use of the courtesy code. I coordinated my program with the Christiansburg Town Council, Police Department and other officials. During the length of the program, participants were taught the National Highway Courtesy Code. The billboard, as depicted on

84

Page 88, carried the simple code, which encouraged drivers to use it.

The results of the study indicated that 97 percent of participants felt less stressed when they used courteous driving behavior. As a result, they developed a more positive attitude toward driving and were less likely to respond violently to events on the road. In short, the program worked.

You can show your community how to become more courteous drivers by teaching children, the next generation of drivers, to actively seek opportunities to be courteous on the highway. By teaching kids how to become safe and courteous drivers, you identify your school with a public need to improve driving conditions. A single act of courtesy has the potential, when paid forward, to change the lives of drivers nationwide. More than just a random act of kindness, these planned and purposeful acts of courtesy can make a definite difference to you and those you teach.

For your benefit, I have organized this communitywide publicity campaign into several easy-to-follow lessons. You have my permission to quote and reproduce any of the information provided about the Road Rage Reducer Project, which is detailed on the following pages.

The Road Rage Reducer Project: Self-Defense on the Highway aka Car-Jitsu

This public-service campaign is designed to teach kids and teens, who will eventually become licensed drivers, how to act when confronted by an aggressive driver in a manner that demonstrates courtesy, discipline and restraint. Martial arts instructors have become experts in teaching courtesy, discipline and restraint. The Road Rage Reducer Project will put our expertise to work in a way that will win public acceptance and build positive public relations in your community.

Every newspaper and radio and TV news program in the country has featured stories about road rage and aggressive driving. Most people expect martial arts instructors to approach aggressive driving from a self-defense perspective. In classical martial arts, you learn to fight so that you can avoid the physical confrontation.

Even though the purpose of classical martial arts is to become adept at killing, the true essence is to also learn how to avoid such extreme action at all costs. The symbolic nature of martial arts is extremely violent, which is why your public-interest campaign must begin with the martial arts most important first lesson: courtesy.

Courtesy is the common denominator that allows a black belt to practice a lethal blow day after day without conflict. Martial artists demonstrate their respect for other people, the art and themselves by being courteous. For example, martial artists bow before and after each confrontation.

How to Become the Resident Road-Rage Expert in Your Community

To develop a successful publicity campaign, you want to become the resident authority and speak at different events. In each case, encourage your market to identify your name and school as the best place to go for martial arts instruction.

As the community's resident expert on courtesy, discipline and restraint, you are now ready to teach some simple truths about road rage and aggressive driving. After becoming familiar with the program, teach the kids at your school. Then send out press releases, and invite the local media to interview you. Create speaking engagements and become the premier community organizer on making highways a friendlier and safer place. Every time you speak or teach about how to use martial arts lessons to combat road rage and aggressive driving, you provide evidence that your school has the community's interest at heart.

I designed the Road Rage Reducer Project specifically for martial arts schools. Every public school, recreation and community service program should be open to having you present the seven-step program. As I mentioned, follow up your work by sending a press release to all media outlets in your area. A copy of a press release specifically for the Road Rage Reducer Project can be found at the conclusion of the chapter.

Necessary Information to Begin Your Publicity Campaign

You will initiate your campaign by teaching the kids in your program the simple seven-step course outline that begins on Page 89. Also, acquaint yourself with the information in this section because it will help you pitch your concept to educators and students. It will also explain why you, as a martial artist, are the community expert on courtesy.

This is your pitch.

Today, our highways are overcrowded, and drivers feel rushed. The general rule for drivers is to get there as fast as you can. If you can be faster or more aggressive than other drivers, you might save a minute or two on your trip. Many people agree that the highways have become war zones.

On the city streets and highways, there are many courteous drivers. It is not uncommon to witness one driver slowing down to allow another to turn into a lane. In a busy parking lot, you often see one driver slow down and motion another driver to freely pull out of a space. These are acts of courtesy. For the most part, they are random and depend on just the right circumstances. Other than throwing up a hand, there is little you can do to acknowledge courteous acts.

Courtesy requires a reward. When you perform a courteous act, such as opening a door for someone or giving up your space in line to accommodate another, you expect a reward. Typically, the reward is a smile of gratitude or a wave of the hand that signifies a thank you. If you continued to open doors and no one responded to your courteous act with a gesture of "thank you," then most likely you would eventually discontinue the courteous behavior.

On the other hand, if you were rewarded every time you performed a courteous act with a reciprocal "thank you," then you most likely would repeat the courteous act as often as possible. Eventually, you would repeat the acts out of habit rather than for the reward. When you perform a courteous act without the need for the reward, then you have performed a "kindness." Courtesy with repeated, reciprocal rewards, leads to kindness. This is how you can take back the highways from aggressive drivers.

Many people have tried to institute a reward method for courteous acts while driving, such as organizing hand gestures, waving hand-held signs or flashing bulky thank-you devices. However, a simpler technology for communicating simple words like "please" and "thank you" is already at your disposal. The common highway hazard lights, often called "flashers" or "blinkers," are intended to communicate that your vehicle is in distress to other drivers. However, it is also easy to control your hazard lights for communicating a simple, courteous code.

To communicate with your hazard lights, follow these steps:

• First, locate the hazard lights in your vehicle while your car is parked.

• Push the button. You will note that the hazard lights will continue to blink until you push the button a second time.

• By turning the lights on and off, you can control the number of blinks that you want other drivers to see.

• Practice sending messages before you attempt to communicate while driving.

The official National Highway Courtesy Code, as illustrated in the picture, is very simple: One blink of the hazard light means "please." Signal "please" when you are asking other drivers to allow your vehicle to enter traffic, when you need to move around a parked car, or when you need to communicate to a vehicle backing out of a parking space that it is safe to proceed. (Note: After the study was completed, the term "blink" was used in place of "flash.")

Perhaps the most often used message continues to be "thank you," which you communicate with two blinks. "Say two for 'thank you' " is the official slogan of the Road Rage Reducer Project. Whenever you are the recipient of a courteous act on the road, push your hazard-lights button. Let the lights blink twice, then turn them off. Practice "say two for thank you" in a parked car so that you will be ready, without effort, to safely "say two for thank you" when needed. When you do "say two for thank you," you will feel as good as the driver who receives the message.

In some cases, you may make a mistake. If you accidentally enter a lane in traffic, pull out too soon into traffic, or stop abruptly to allow a pedestrian to cross, you can signal with three blinks for "I am sorry." Of course, a bad maneuver on the road is no excuse, but it often helps to acknowledge a wrongful act.

Finally, if you are in distress or need help, communicate to others by blinking your hazard lights four times followed by a pause. Repeat this pattern until assistance arrives. When others see that you are attempting to signal a message, they will be more likely to respond than if they see that your hazard lights are randomly flashing.

How can people help? By using the code on the road. Tell family and friends about the official National Highway Courtesy Code. Teach others. I've designed a seven-step course outline so that teachers and student leaders can enlist children to encourage adults to become courteous drivers. Kids who join the program are called "Road Rage Rangers." When properly trained, kids can teach their parents and others to be more courteous on the highways. Later, when Road Rage Rangers become adult drivers, they will most likely continue to practice the courteous gestures that they have grown up with.

Kids are going to learn about driving through the gestures they see adults perform. Let's make sure kids see courteous drivers. The next generation of drivers is being trained today. Let's make sure that they are trained to be courteous drivers. Many highways are crowded and in desperate need of a social change from aggression to kindness. Please help.

The information in your program targets three different age groups: kids who are called "Road Rage Rangers," teenagers who are called "Road Rage Riders," and licensed drivers who are referred to as "Road Rage Reducers." Remember, you will teach the lessons to groups made up of all three kinds of people, so your discussion should engage them accordingly.

Outline for Presenting the Road Rage Rangers Program

Try the program in your martial arts school before taking the campaign to other locations. You will be the "leader." As students get their parents involved, record any positive responses. At the completion of the seven-step program, contact your local paper. To teach the program, just follow the outline. I also recommend that you practice teaching each lecture topic to your students.

Lesson 1

Lecture: Have you ever heard about highway bullies? They are drivers who use their cars or trucks to take advantage of others. I am a driver, and I see it all the time. When people drive too fast, swoop in and out of lanes, tailgate or drive too slowly to prevent others from passing, they are using their cars to bully others.

Discussion: What behaviors have you seen on the highways?

Lecture: This bullylike behavior is called "aggressive driving." When a driver purposefully tries to endanger others, it is called "road rage." Road rage and aggressive driving are patterns of rude behavior. It is an epidemic in our country, and it's against the law.

Discussion: Have you ever been in a car while a Road Rage Rudee— a "rudee" is someone who is rude on the highway—was driving? I have a new program to help stop road rage and aggressive driving by promoting courtesy on the highways. It's called the Road Rage Ranger Project, and it was started by a martial arts instructor because martial artists always try to be courteous. In the next few lessons, you'll learn more about the program and how you can become a Road Rage Ranger. If kids across the country get together, they can change the way people drive. They can help make the highways more safe and friendly. Are you interested?

Note to Leader: Be aware that parents often are the Road Rage Rudees in a child's life.

Lesson 2

Lecture: If you are frightened, uncomfortable or feel like a victim when an adult exhibits behavior like yelling at other drivers, driving too fast, tailgating, running red lights, and swooping in and out of lanes, you need to voice your opinion. Tell the adult driver that you studied this type of behavior in your class. These aggressive or angry drivers are called Road Rage Rudees. Say to the driver, "You're becoming a Road Rage Rudee." When confronted with a bully or a rude person, never keep your feelings inside. Talk to others about how that type of behavior makes you feel.

Discussion: How does rude and dangerous behavior make you feel? The ensuing discussion might naturally include school or neighborhood bullies. As the team leader, you should consider all discussion valid, but try to return to the topic of highway bullies.

Assignment: Ask the students to keep a list of driving behaviors that scare them or make them uncomfortable. Ask them to observe other drivers and keep a list of times when other drivers act aggressively. Finally, request that the kids ask their parents or other adult drivers if they have ever been the victims of a Road Rage Rudee.

Note to Leader: Be prepared to collect the lists for discussion in the next class.

Lesson 3

Lecture: After reading our lists from last class and talking about them, I think we can all agree that it is sometimes dangerous on the highways when drivers become Road Rage Rudees and drive aggressively. Did you know that road rage and aggressive driving are considered an epidemic?

Discussion: What can we do to stop Road Rage Rudees and dangerous, aggressive drivers?

Lecture: Laws have been passed to make acts of road rage a criminal offense. Police have been schooled in how to identify aggressive drivers, but what can you do?

A study was conducted at Radford University in which participants were asked to focus their attention on being courteous drivers instead of acting aggressively. Drivers in the study were instructed to use their hazard lights as a communication tool to tell other drivers "please," "thank you" and "I'm sorry." A professor designed a code in which one blink means "please," like when you are trying to merge into traffic. Two blinks means "thank you," which replaces waving your hand—a gesture sometimes mistaken for aggressive intent. You can also use the signal for "thank you" when another driver slows down to let you in the same lane or when someone gives up a parking space for you. If you make a mistake, like almost pulling into someone's lane or not slowing down in time, give the code of three blinks for "I am sorry."

Note to Leader: Distribute the Road Rage Rangers decal or some other kind of badge. The Road Rage Rangers and Road Rage Riders are kids who help instruct adults to demonstrate, look for and reward courteous acts on the highways.

Assignment: Tell the students to ask their parents to demonstrate the hazard-light signals in their car while parked. Tell the students to teach their parents the National Highway Courtesy Code and place their Road Rage Rangers decal or badge on the back window of their car to let people know that they are in training to become a courteous driver.

Note to Leader: Make fliers for the kids to take home that explain to their parents how to use the code, how to locate the hazard lights on a vehicle, and why it is important to be courteous on the road, just like it is important to be courteous in class, in public and in life.

At this point in the program, you need to begin sending out e-mails like newsletters to spread information on the National Highway Courtesy Code. Encourage readers to stop by your school and pick up a free pamphlet or flier that explains the code and how your students are learning the importance of being courteous on the highways. Ask your local auto-insurance representatives if they will help sponsor the program by contributing the funds to print pamphlets or fliers. Agree to carry the names of the sponsors on the fliers.

Lesson 4

Lecture: The first lesson in martial arts is courtesy. In martial arts classes, you engage in dangerous skills that, if not controlled, could result in injury and even death. On the highways, drivers engage in common behaviors, such as using their vehicles to turn, pass and stop. These behaviors, if not controlled, can result in injury or death.

In martial arts, you practice courtesy as a code of behavior, such as bowing to an opponent or only using your skills in life-threatening situations. To improve safety on the highways and to stop road rage and aggressive driving, you must learn to practice courtesy!

Discussion: How many of you can remember a situation in which a driver was courteous?

Assignment: Now that the students have shown their parents the National Highway Courtesy Code, encourage them to be on the lookout for any courteous act, such as when someone lets them merge into traffic. When they see the act, encourage them to "say two for thank you." Have them keep a record of instances in which a driver used the code and was able to communicate "thank you."

Note to Leader: At the end of lesson four, take the results of your program to the local media and let them know how members of your martial arts school have joined in the effort to participate in planned and purposeful acts of courtesy. Continue to promote the code through mass e-mails and word-of-mouth discussions. When people in your community know the code, they will know what to look for when engaging in a courteous act. It starts with a few drivers, and through your efforts, you can cover an entire community in a few weeks.

Lesson 5

Lecture: Courtesy requires a reward. If I am courteous to you, then I expect you to say "thank you." Have you ever done something nice for another person, like stopping to open a door? Does that person usually say "thank you?" How did it make you feel? Very good, right? Because the person repaid your courteous behavior with the grateful gesture, it made you want to do it again. You learn to open doors for others, assist others in simple tasks like helping someone into a car, carrying in groceries or sharing an umbrella. When you are nice to others, others are nice to you. Courtesy is catching!

When you practice courteous acts, you serve as a model to others who, in turn, become courteous. When drivers actively set out to be courteous on the highway, they lose any sense of anger or aggression. As more and more drivers participate in the program, they can actually change the way they drive.

Discussion: Ask the students to describe courteous acts that they've performed on the highways. Then lead them to the following thought: Usually, you signal "thank you" by waving a hand, but at night, this method doesn't work because it's too dark. Explain how the National Highway Courtesy Code was developed to solve this problem.

Note to Leader: Most discussions will not be about highway courtesy. Try to link nonhighway acts of courtesy to similar acts that may occur on the highway.

Assignment: Your students might remember a popular movie called *Pay It Forward*. The theme of the movie was to do something kind for someone else. The mission of Road Rage Rangers/Riders is to teach others to be courteous on the highways. Encourage students to tell others that they have joined the Road Rage Rangers/Riders and that their mission is to teach others how to use the National Highway Courtesy Code. Because you've taught them that courtesy requires a reward, it becomes the student's responsibility as a Road Rage Ranger/Rider to teach others to be courteous and to reward courteous acts by using the National Highway Courtesy Code.

Lesson 6

Lecture: Instruct the kids in your program to continue keeping records of confirmed courteous acts on the highways. Tell the students that as soon as their adult driver has participated in a minimum of 10 acts of courtesy—including incidents in which they have been courteous or have been the recipients of courteous acts—they can award that driver with a Certified Courteous Driver decal or other badge to place on the rear window of a vehicle. Provide a take-home flier with the extra-credit assignment and select team members for participation.

Assignment: Record all acts of courtesy on the highways, and submit the names of adult drivers who you believe deserve the Certified Courteous Driver award.

Extra-Credit Assignment: Participate in a team Highway Courtesy Challenge. Over the course of two weeks, invite drivers to earn points for courteous acts. Award three points for each behavior, or develop your own point system. Here are some ideas:

- slowing to allow another driver to enter a lane
  (If the act takes place in commuter traffic, add two points.)
- stopping to allow pedestrians to move at a crosswalk
- using the National Highway Courtesy Code

- stopping to allow another driver the right of way, at a four-way stop, for example
- refusing to allow angry, aggressive thoughts to influence the driver's actions
- stopping to allow another driver to pull out of a parking space
- developing a habit of always using turn signals properly
- choosing not to use a cell phone while driving

Lose three points for the following behaviors:

- swooping between lanes
- tailgating
- failing to slow down at a yellow light
- speeding up beyond the flow of traffic
- using the horn or lights in an aggressive manner
- using any hand gesture that may be aggressive
- yelling at other drivers
- becoming distracted by cell phones, radios, etc.

At the end of the two-week challenge, have all participants tally the scores and award the title of "Certified Courteous Driver" to the winning participant. The Highway Courtesy Challenge is best presented when you have several teams of one to six kids—representing six families—on a team, competing for the award.

Note to Leader: While teaching this program, you have no doubt engaged in the process of becoming a courteous driver. To recognize your commitment to changing the way you drive—from aggression and danger to courtesy and safety—award yourself the official Certified Courteous Driver decal (free to instructors at www.roadragereducer.org). Place it on your back window.

Lesson 7: Graduation

Lecture: This is how the Road Rage Reducer Project began. A driver was traveling on a busy interstate highway. It had been raining most of the day. It was dark, and it was hard to see the highway signs clearly. At the last minute, the young driver saw the sign for his exit. He was in the left lane, and the right lane was filled with bumper-to-bumper traffic. He was nervous about getting into the other lane to make his exit. A courteous driver, seeing the young man's dilemma, slowed and motioned for him to merge. The young driver made the turn and was thankful. He threw up his hand to say "thank you," but it went unnoticed. The rain and darkness made it impossible to say "thank you." The young driver never forgot that act of courtesy. He went on to develop the National Highway Courtesy Code and this program.

Discussion: Talk about how the students have learned that courteous acts lead to kindness and how they should pay it forward and pass it on.

Note to Leader: At the programs end, celebrate your students' achievements with a graduation ceremony. Offer thoughts to the students and their parents that reflect their committment to courtesy.

Continuing Your Road Rage Reducer Publicity Campaign

You will discover that public-school groups and others will gladly welcome you to teach this program. Why? Because it is in the public's interest to stop aggressive driving. Every driver has been the victim or target of an aggressive driver. All drivers have wished that they could do something about road rage. Every driver has experienced the highway bully.

It takes three weeks to conclude the program. The program is concluded when the participants get their parents or drivers to think about road courtesy at every opportunity. At the conclusion of the program, ask students to pose for a photo. Send the photo along with a press release to every media outlet in your area. Be prepared for follow-up interviews. When I first offered the program, my partner and I were bombarded with requests for interviews. We received local, regional and national coverage.

As you become identified as the "road rage" expert in your community, work with town and city administrators to establish a community courtesy day. You can hold car washes, bake sales and other fundraisers to pay for printed copies of the program to distribute to others. You may want to buy business cards, bumper stickers and other promotional materials. Because you are an expert in courtesy, it makes sense to promote this concept in your community. Everyone appreciates courteous acts.

Press Release for the Road Rage Reducer Project

It might be a good idea to include a quote from a student, praising the program. An example quote is as follows: "My mom has stopped yelling at other drivers and started looking for ways to be courteous. She slows down to let others get in front of her, and she thanks people all the time now. I get to blink the lights for her."

Feel free to use the following press release when making your own:

For Immediate Release

Karate Kids Teach Lessons on Highway Courtesy

Anywhere, USA (December 8, 2008)—Researchers say that some of the most aggressive driving on the road is demonstrated by drivers of vans, usually crammed with kids. The drivers often are called "soccer moms." Now the kids are being taught how to transform aggressive drivers into courtesy drivers.

Twelve students graduated from the Road Rage Rangers program here recently. The program was presented by (fill in your school name) to help combat the incidence of aggressive driving and road rage on the highways. Participants in the program were taught the National Highway Courtesy Code, which can be communicated by using the hazard lights located on the control panel of a car. Drivers can say "thank you" by blinking the hazard lights twice. Kids in the program earn points when they teach their parents to be courteous drivers and to use the courtesy code. (Fill in your name here) tells students that "the first lesson in martial arts is about courtesy. To practice potentially lethal blows without injury requires trust, discipline and respect. You bow to your partner to show respect for a courteous act. On the highway, each driver has a potentially dangerous vehicle. What you didn't have until now was a way to tell other drivers 'thank you' for your kind act."

The Road Rage Reducer program teaches drivers to use hazard lights to send coded messages for "thank you" (two blinks) and "sorry" (three blinks), which comes in handy if the driver makes a mistake.

For more information, please contact (place your school information here).

Keeping the Community Involved

Depending on the level of success of your first program, you may be able to get businesses to contribute prizes and other support for future programs. Monetary support can be used for developing advertisements that encourage interested readers to contact your school to begin the next program. Each person you meet can help promote your school. When you get the public to associate your school with acts of kindness and courtesy, you build positive publicity and make an honest effort to help others.

The school owner who masters the art of publicity and who works daily to create and reinforce a positive image will enjoy much success. Remember, public relations is a continuous process. Work each day to promote your community-service Road Rage Reducer Project and continue to gain public acceptance for your school.

CHAPTER 7

SALES PROMOTIONS

SALES PROMOTIONS

general and seasonal promotions • effective tactics • scripted calls

Sales promotions are an incentive that encourages the prospect to take action now and are a fundamental task for every successful car dealership, professional team franchise and martial arts studio. For martial arts instructors, they create excitement, generate interest and bring potential members to visit their school. They motivate visitors and prospects to become members.

Because a sales promotion usually has an expiration date—a set time when the offer will no longer be valid—there is an implied urgent call to action, now! We have each waited on items to "go on sale" before buying. Smart buyers look for the "blue-light specials," "red-tag sale" or "markdowns." Think of the sales promotion as that extra incentive.

The Top 22 Sales Promotions

While one promotion may work in your area, another could fail. I knew a sales trainer who frequently asked the question, "Have you tried selling ice to the Eskimos?" His point was that people do not buy something if they do not perceive a need for it. When you make the need for your product clear and match it with the perfect sales promotion, you will have a winner.

Here are some proven promotions that work in schools across the country:

1. All-Day, All-Night Workout

i. Invite members to bring guests to participate in an all-day workout. Present different clinics, speakers, programs about weight loss, new techniques, etc. The key is to encourage and impress the guests so that they will want to become members. Programs for kids are a natural for all-night workouts, or lock-ins. (Lock the doors after hours so parents know exactly where their kids are and what they will be doing.) You can charge a fee for the kids' overnight camp. Usually, parents are happy to have their children spend the night in a fun, safe environment away from home.

ii. Generate leads for the sleepover through your current members. Plan at least a month in advance. Let parents know the dates, costs and what the child will be doing. Generate discussion in the kids' classes to build up interest in the sleepover. Award each child who brings a friend with a gift. Often, the value of the gift determines how hard the children and parents will try to bring in guests.

iii. Make the program so much fun that the new child will want to come back for a free week of instruction. A sleepover will help the new child become acquainted with your school and give you the opportunity to learn about the new child's needs so you can create the perfect sales pitch.

2. Pick a Balloon

i. Put the name of a grand prize in a balloon. Place balloons around the entranceway to the club. Every balloon will have a slip of paper with a small reward. A few balloons will have the names of larger prizes. The value of the prize will greatly influence your members' participation. Members either invite guests or provide names and phone numbers for a referral.

ii. When a guest becomes a member, the person who recruited the new member gets to pick a balloon. Remember, the success of the promotion often depends on the prizes. Inexpensive prizes usually result in moderate success. Some interesting gifts may include a one-year subscription to *Black Belt*, free movie tickets or a free pass for a rank exam. Ask your students for suggestions.

3. Grab Bags

i. The grab-bag promotion is similar to the balloon idea. Students recruit potential members, then the names of those who sign up as a result of the promotion are placed in a bag. At the end of the two-week promotion, draw the name from the bag to award the prize to the new member and the student who made the referral.

ii. For the grab-bag promotion to be effective, you must create and maintain a constant and continuous interest in the promotion. Run the promotion for one month and have weekly drawings. Create some degree of drama as you reach into the bag and pull out the name of the winner. The winners will help create excitement for the promotion. Excitement and the value of the prize can make the promotion a great success.

4. One-Day Class Drawing

i. Ask members to invite guests to the class for a one-day promotion. The names of guests and their recruiters are entered into a drawing. Draw a name from the fishbowl to determine the winner. Again, the prize value affects the participation level.

5. Guest Passes

i. Guess passes resemble business cards and offer two to four weeks of free instruction. Be sure to note that prospects are allowed only one guest pass. Otherwise, prospects might collect several cards for months of free lessons. Carry lots of cards and give them out at every opportunity.

6. Video-Store Promotion

i. Check with your local video stores. Ask clerks to hand out free guest passes to anyone renting martial arts movies. If you know the owner, ask whether you can attach a sticker stating "free martial arts lessons with rental" on the video box. Make your card and offer attractive, and you will improve the results of the promotion. Getting the video-store clerks excited can improve the promotion. You may choose to run this promotion only for new and well-advertised martial-arts-themed movies.

7. Hotel/Motel Promotion

i. Many hotels and motels cannot afford to manage a fitness program on the premises. Few if any have a room available for martial arts. Offer to make your school available to their guests as part of the amenities package offered at check-in. In exchange, you might be able to barter for lodging. Also, guests might purchase souvenirs and other products from your school. If you are hosting a seminar or summer camp that might attract interest beyond your region, offer to promote the hotel or motel as the primary location for lodging in return for one or more nights of free lodging.

8. Discounts for Day Classes

i. In many martial arts schools, "prime time" is after 5 p.m. You can lower fees to encourage morning and afternoon use of your facility. There is a growing market for home-schooled kids and for pre-schoolers. To introduce an early morning program, consider doing a discount promotion for daytime classes. A lunchtime fitness program also can be developed using this promotion.

9. Summer Discounts

i. Typically, summer is a slow, low-use period for many schools because kids and adults like to do things outdoors and take vacations. Try a summer discount. Offer 50 percent off to prospects who sign up for three months. You might also incorporate this promotion with your summer camp by providing an additional discount to people who sign up for both.

10. Shopping Center/Mall Booths

i. Construct a simple booth where you can leave your advertising and promotional materials, like brochures and sign-up sheets, for patrons to pick up as they shop. Decorate the booth's walls with your display materials. You can also just set up a table and have someone at your school sit behind it. Obviously, the best time to set up the booth or table is when there are a lot of people at the mall. This can be very effective during the back-to-school and Christmas shopping seasons. You may also be able to rent a booth for a month. Often, these satellite programs serve the purpose of doubling your potential to meet and greet new prospects.

11. Karate Parties

i. Kids enjoy getting together to celebrate a friend's birthday. Encourage younger students to host birthday parties at your school. To add to the appeal, offer prizes, games and a free lesson. Those attending will become acquainted with your school. You want people to know about your school and think that your school is the martial arts epicenter of your area. Karate parties can be a great way to attract positive attention.

12. Lead Boxes

i. Boxes for leads, as in prospects, can be purchased commercially and decorated with your photo or logo. Put up lead boxes everywhere. Many locally owned businesses are open to the idea of placing lead boxes in their lobbies, while most franchise stores no longer permit it. Ask your school members for referrals. The lead box will have an application form that states something like, "Win a free week of martial arts lessons!" Usually, people who sign and place their names in the box are good leads. Call each applicant to set up a visit. Review the section about using the phone, and use the script for outgoing calls. This is discussed later on in the chapter.

13. Free Clinic

i. Offer a free demonstration or instructional class to target particular groups. Self-defense for kids and aerobic kickboxing for adults are class-topic examples. Put up fliers, send press releases and ask members to tell others about the free class.

14. Join Now at Last Year's Rates

i. Often, you hear about car dealers who offer the same promotion, so this sales pitch should be self-explanatory. If not, the message it sends is that if a prospect signs up for a class before deadline, then the prospect saves money. This promotion works well as a January/February promotion.

15. Direct-Mail Marketing (Including E-mail)

i. Collect e-mail addresses. The addresses can be generated from your member base or perhaps from members of a school that has recently gone out of business. Ask members to share their e-mail lists with you. Use the e-mail list to educate your market. In brief monthly installments, spotlight a school member. In the student's own words, let the member describe how he or she has lost weight, earned belts, improved his or her outlook on life, etc. Let parents describe how martial arts training has helped their child do better in school, defeat a bully or become more respectful. On occasion, you may review a martial arts movie or address self-defense choices, compare martial arts or compare your art to another. Make each topic current, brief and to the point. Conclude each message with a free offer for one or more weeks of instruction, or simply invite the reader to a free demo at your school. Send the e-mails on a regular basis, and allow people receiving the message to opt out of receiving additional e-mails.

ii. Often, professional marketers use direct-mail marketing of hard-copy coupon books and fliers. For a fee—usually less than $300, depending on the number of copies being printed—a professional marketing company will mail your coupon along with many others, ranging from theater tickets to car repairs. These coupon books are sent to every postal address in your community. Make the offer attractive enough to get the person to visit your school. Follow up with a motivational class and do a superb job of selling your product. Then maximize your earning potential with an e-mail marketing campaign.

16. Join Now and Get the Summer Free

i. This promotion is useful for early spring campaigns. Because summer is typically slow, you can afford to give away summer tuition as an incentive for prospective clients to sign up now. The student signs a contract for the regular 12-month instructional program, and you waive payment for June, July and August.

17. 99 Days for $99

i. Primarily thought of as a summer promotion, this is an effective way to provide an incentive for new students to sign up during slow periods. It's hardly worth taking out a newspaper advertisement for this promotion. Make fliers and display the promotion in the front window of your school.

18. Two-for-One Initiation Fee

i. To encourage a prospect to bring along a friend or family member, offer two membership sign-up fees for the price of one. Everyone wants to save money. The concept of selling two memberships and charging only one membership initiation (usually $100 to $150) originated with professional health clubs.

19. Halloween Parties

i. Kids love to attend Halloween parties. To make your Halloween party successful, the kids have to bring guests. Halloween is the perfect time of the year to host a ninja costume party. The kids wear ninja costumes and disguise their faces with face paint. You can have a "best costume" contest. Many of the kids will be motivated to purchase ninja uniforms from your pro shop before the party.

a. Add to the ninja theme by organizing an obstacle course. Design your course so that students must climb over, under and through temporary obstacles. You may even be able to charge an entry fee for the competitions. When you make these promotions fun and exciting, guests are more apt to come back to your school for instruction. Even if they don't, they may tell other people how much fun your school is.

b. Once you begin the theme parties, you can follow up with a St. Patrick's Day party—every child gets to put green coloring on their hair or decorate their uniforms with the color green— and other fun event days.

20. Word of Mouth/Each One Reach One

i. The goal of this promotion is to get members and staff to talk to others. No selling or coaxing is needed. No lists are generated, and no prizes are offered. Just ask members to pledge to talk to one or more new people each day and tell them why they love martial arts at your school. This is a year-round campaign, and it is the primary sales promotion used by some highly successful clubs. If you do make the "each one reach one" campaign a fundamental promotional tool, consider having an end-of-the-year banquet to recognize students who recruited the most prospects.

ii. Promotions like this one work well for large schools but are less effective for the smaller ones because they don't have as many student recruiters. The more students you get involved, the more successful your promotional campaign can become.

21. Open House/Grand Opening

i. You would be surprised to learn that less than half of all martial arts schools have grand-opening events. If you missed your grand-opening opportunity, you still can hold an open house at least once a year. The benefits include tremendous PR promotions and opportunities to identify prospects and sell memberships.

ii. Offering recruitment incentives to your members will make your open houses more effective. Send press releases to local news-papers, and complement the release with a display in your front window. Your goal is to get as many people to visit your school as possible and convert those visits into memberships.

iii. Dress up your school. Make sure that all facilities are clean, unclut-tered, and that members and staff are ready for the big event. Remember, your goal is to get as many guests as possible to attend the event. Plan programs that will entertain, educate and motivate visitors to become members. Here are some ideas:

  a. Host a small, multievent tournament or consider a break-a-thon, kick-a-thon or punch-a-thon.

  b. Offer women's self-defense programs, and make it free to the public. Self-defense programs for kids are just as successful.

  c. Plan a first-rate team demonstration. Train your kids and adults in a special demonstration. Parents love to attend kids' demos.

  d. Invite guest speakers for seminars. Invite an author, champion or master to provide a seminar.

  e. Invite a band. Many kids and adults belong to bands. Most will play a few songs for no charge.

  f. Hire a radio-station crew. Find out whether it is cost-effective to hire the crew to perform a "remote" broadcast at your event.

22. Self-Defense Awareness Surveys

i. Surveys do several things: They inform others about the need for taking self-defense classes, and they also get word out about your school. To construct your own survey, simply develop five to 10 questions that suit your preference, school and goals. Conduct the survey at shopping malls, via telephone or by going door to door. Many of the survey participants will want to talk at length about safety and self-defense. Be positive and encouraging. Help the individual by eventually getting him or her to come visit your school and participate in a free class. There is an example of a survey in Appendix A.

Because members play an important role in the success of your program, prepare your students with the proper information to promote your event. The timing of the promotion should coincide with peak buying times to be most effective. Poor media selection, lack of creativity and poor location also can negatively affect your promotions. If your club has a quality public image and your facilities are first-rate, you increase your odds for success. The cost of your free prize and its value to the prospects play a large role in the success of your promotion, but ultimately, you control the factors that determine whether your promotion is a success.

Seasonal Promotions

As with most businesses, the martial arts school operation has certain peaks and valleys similar to those in the fitness field. Peak times include September's back-to-school phase and the New Year's resolution phase. There are four discernible buying patterns. Spend your advertising dollars when buying times are strong.

January to March

For most fitness-related programs, the first-of-the-year buying cycle is the strongest. Many Americans still make promises to get in shape or learn something new each New Year's. The result is a definite surge in visits to martial arts schools. Invest your time and advertising dollars in an open-house promotion.

Back to School

Most Americans associate the fall months with going back to school. Adults seem more interested in learning new programs in the fall. Parents are apt to include martial arts instruction with their children's back-to-school activities. Any of the party ideas are a good choice. Don't hesitate to purchase display ads, such as bumper stickers and posters, for back-to-school programs.

Spring

During the spring, there's an influx of potential students who are interested in getting in shape for the summer. However, newspaper advertisements are less effective during spring unless they are promoting summer-camp programs. Begin your summer-camp advertisements in late May or early June about two or three weeks before the end of school.

Summer

Traditionally, summer is the least active buying cycle for martial arts schools, but summer-camp programs have greatly increased summer business. The general approach is to recruit children to participate in martial arts instruction and offer general supervision for four to eight hours a day, which is appealing to working parents. Often, these programs provide a lunch. Other activities such as swimming, field trips and other outdoor events can be integrated into the program. The key to running a successful martial arts summer camp is to continually change activities throughout the day.

Other summer promotions include "99 days for $99 dollars" or "sign up now for one year and get the summer free." Remember, get the most from your investment by buying ads primarily during peak seasons.

Factors That Increase the Effectiveness of Promotions

To hold a successful promotion, consider any potential advertising and PR opportunities, then train your employees so they know exactly how to answer the phone, greet visitors and teach new members. If you are the only employee at your school, this means that you are the publicity specialist, sales manager, advertising executive and creative genius behind each promotion. But no matter who is involved, all areas—public relations, advertising, etc.—must come together to create a successful promotion.

When I opened my first full-time studio many years ago, I selected a lead-box campaign combined with a mall display and mall demonstration as my first sales promotion. The mall manager gave me two weeks to run my promotion. I constructed a booth with a drop box so that customers could fill out a card and drop it in the box. There were photos of my school and students on the display boards. The "grand prize" included a karate T-shirt, a ninja uniform and a television. Every applicant won a free week of instruction.

The information provided in the mall display stated that I would hold a drawing on January 25 and provide a martial arts demonstration. Every night for two weeks leading up to the final day of the promotion, I would stop by the mall at closing time, take out all the applications for the day and sort through the cards.

I averaged 40 to 50 cards per day. For every 50 cards, only 25 were good leads. Some people would fill out two or more cards. Some applicants were from different states, just visiting the mall. The leads I selected had to be within 10 miles from my studio to be considered good prospects.

After sorting through the leads, I would call the next evening between 5:30 p.m. and 6:30 p.m. During the call, I informed the prospects that their names had been entered into the January 25 drawing and that they had won a free week of instruction at my school. I was surprised to discover that some people dropped the phone or screamed in excitement, "I won!"

For every 30 calls, I would average 15 appointments. Out of 15 confirmed appointments, seven or more prospects would show up for class. While I averaged an 80 percent show-up rate from my first promotion, I could count on at least half of all the people who took a free class to sign a contract to continue instruction.

I combined my lead-box promotion with weekend newspaper advertisements, fliers posted all over town and around the mall, and a word-of-mouth campaign by my students. More than 100 spectators came to the mall demonstration, and 500 applicants were collected during the two-week period. Two hundred calls led to 100 confirmed appointments, and the free lessons yielded 52 new students in the month of January for my school.

The cost for the promotion prizes was less than $100. Almost all my new students signed contracts for the Black Belt Program. I netted $50,000 in contracts for a $100 investment. My school was located in a small college town with less than 20,000 permanent residents and less than 15,000 college students. A well-constructed sales promotion, which includes successful advertising, demos, phone follow-ups and personal selling, can greatly increase the number of students at your school and return a considerable profit.

The Phone

A few years ago, the public generally accepted promotional calls from health clubs and martial arts studios. This is no longer true. If you use your phone to solicit a response, be sure to have a well-thought-out script and stick to it. The script is just as important when receiving incoming calls to your studio, too.

Instead of just saying, "Hello," try this: "We're having a great day at (your school name)," or "Thank you for calling (your school name)." Be positive and upbeat. Inform the caller with, "I'll be glad to help you." Your goal is to persuade the caller to visit your school. Provide the caller with correct information, and gently guide the caller into setting an appointment time.

Ask the caller, "Are you familiar with our school?" Offer to tell the caller more about your programs. Often, you can schedule an appointment by providing available time slots. For example, say, "I have an opening on Monday at 5 p.m. or on Tuesday at 4:30 p.m. Which is better for you?" Typically, the caller will make a choice. Repeat the time, and provide directions to your school. Invite the caller to bring a friend.

Tips for Making Your Phone Conversations More Effective

When people call your school, it is almost always because they are interested in taking lessons from you. It's up to you to follow a script and provide the information that leads to an appointment. In order to help a caller sign up for lessons, you must first meet this prospective client. The phone provides an excellent tool for encouraging callers to visit your facilities.

Develop a script.

A script is an organized dialogue between you and the caller. By following a professionally designed script, you increase your chances of providing the correct information and collecting enough contact info to make a follow-up call.

Prepare in advance to receive phone calls.

Train individuals who answer the phone at your school on how to properly obtain information from the caller.

Callers do not like to be put on hold.

If you must put a caller on hold, check back every 10 to 20 seconds. Callers appreciate it when you provide the exact information they require. This is why the call must be handled by a person who understands how to properly receive a call. Answer the phone confidently. Remember, the caller contacted you because he or she needs help.

As you respond to the caller, demonstrate both your concern for his or her request and excitement for your program. The phone call is often the caller's first introduction to your school. Demonstrate your professional training by handling the call in a courteous, informative manner.

Every call should have a conclusion.

By following your script, you will be able to inform the caller and collect information, including his or her name, how he or she heard about your school, and when the caller would like to visit your school for a free lesson.

When used effectively, the telephone can lead to the successful recruitment of new students. If you take away your telephone or waste recruitment time with ineffective conversations, you severely limit your ability to attract potential members. If you have only a few seconds via the telephone with potential members, make them count.

The Script for Incoming Calls

There are eight components that should be addressed when designing a professional phone script for incoming calls.

1. "Thank you for calling."

After picking up the phone, smile and greet the customer with, "Thank you for calling (insert the name of your school)." Some schools prefer the greeting, "We're having a great day at (insert your school name)! How may I help you?"

Why smile? Try this test. Make a frown. Lower your eyebrows and squint your eyes. Say, "Thank you for calling." Now smile big. Show some smiley teeth. Say, "Thank you for calling." Which is easier? When you are smiling, the attitude comes through. The idea is to sound excited to receive the prospect's call. Smile.

2. "I'll be glad to help you."

Regardless of how the caller responds to your entry, say the words, "I'll be glad to help you." By taking control of the conversation, you ensure that the caller gets the correct information. Remember that many callers will be anxious about calling a martial arts school. Often, people think that even though they would like to learn martial arts, they could be injured or embarrassed by taking classes. You have to put them at ease.

3. "By the way, my name is (your name here). May I ask yours?"

By repeating this line, you make the caller feel more comfortable. Use the person's name during the conversation.

4. "Are you familiar with our club?"

Remember, the caller might be anxious and probably does not understand enough about martial arts to know what to ask. If you offer multiple programs, the caller most likely will not be aware of them all. The question is intended to get to the point of the call.

5. "Let me tell you a little about our club."

If you are running a special ad or promotion, you might want to mention something about that specific program first. You may want to say, "Our club was started in (year) and has been a leader in the martial arts community since that time. We are certified by (provide information) to offer expert instruction in (be specific)." Let's say that you are a certified taekwondo instructor. Your next line would be, "Have you ever practiced taekwondo?" At this point, the caller will confirm whether he or she is calling because he or she has an interest in taekwondo.

6. "I would like to set up an appointment."

Ultimately, the caller is interested in taking instruction from you, and that is the reason for the call. Give the caller a choice. Say, "I have an opening for Tuesday at 5 p.m. or Wednesday at 6 p.m. Which is best for you?" By providing an alternate choice, you have made it easier for the caller to make a decision.

7. "How did you find out about our program?"

Once callers schedule their appointments to visit your school, ask them how they heard about you. By doing so, you can determine whether the call represents a referral, is the result of an ad or promotion, or the person is simply a new prospect.

8. Repeat four things at the conclusion of the call.

Conclude the call by repeating the location of your studio and the time of his or her appointment. Also, repeat the person's name and extend an invitation to bring a friend. Many people prefer to attend the first class with someone they know. As an added bonus, you now have two prospects.

Outgoing Calls

Once you have been running promotions for a while, you will have a list of names of prospects to call, and you will need a script to effectively contact them. Here's a generic but effective one between a school owner named "Mike" and a prospect named "Lora":

Owner: Hi. This is Mike with Acme Martial Arts. May I please speak to Lora?
Prospect: This is Lora.

Owner: Hi, Lora. I am calling to let you know that, as a result of our June 2 drawing, you have been selected to receive two weeks of free instruction at our school.
Prospect: Wow, that's great!

Owner: Lora, you'll be able to participate in any of our programs and use the facility as often as you like during your free visits. I would like to set you up for your first visit. I have an opening on Monday at 5 p.m. or Tuesday at 6 p.m. Which is better for you?
Prospect: Monday at 5p.m. sounds good.

Owner: Great. Lora, I'll be expecting you on Monday, (insert date) at 5 p.m. Ask for me, Mike, when you come in. Just wear something comfortable, and if you like, you can bring a friend.
Prospect: Thank you. See you then!

Mike did not waste time during the conversation. He provided the details upfront. He offered Lora a choice. Having the choice of time allowed Lora to make a quick decision. At the end of the conversation, Mike repeated the details and expectations.

You can add or delete components of the script for outgoing calls with whatever you think is necessary. You'll need to practice the script many times before you can say it naturally. You must control the subject and direction of the call to collect the information in an efficient and productive manner. Using a carefully designed script will provide you with a continuous stream of prospects/potential students.

The Hot Box

While taking each call, write the prospect's name, reason for the visit, time of the visit, and contact information on a form. Purchase a weekly file or a plastic file box to place the cards in. The file becomes your "hot box." In the hot box, organize prospective appointments based on the day they arrive at your school for each day of the week. Constantly follow up leads and set up appointments for each caller who contacts your school. Many calls will come from continuous promotions, advertising or publicity.

On any given day, you should be able to open your office door, go to your hot box, and verify who will be showing up for instruction in the appropriate classes. A full hot box will mean that your promotional efforts are paying off. An empty hot box means that you need to do more work promoting your school.

When prospective students visit your school for the first time, find out how you can help them and how much they can afford to pay for instruction. Think of your school as a hospital. A patient comes in. The patient must be checked in. A history for that patient must be taken in order to determine the best way that the patient may be served by the hospital.

Martial arts students have all sorts of wants and needs. In order to serve prospective students, present an organized and detailed program to discover their needs. Such an assessment includes the following:

- the best time for the student to take instruction
- the immediate goals for the person (weight loss, self-defense, etc.)
- why the person selected your school
- any person who the prospective student must consult before signing up for lessons at your school
- the prospect's place of employment

We will discuss this assessment process in greater detail in the next chapter called personal selling and commitment counseling.

Why You Teach

Some teachers complain that using a script and these tactics is entrapment. These teachers argue, "I didn't get into martial arts to become a salesperson." As a result, there will be hundreds of individuals in their community who miss out on the life-changing benefits of martial arts because the instructors didn't reach out to them.

If you're like most instructors, you have spent years enjoying the benefits of practicing a martial art. Wouldn't you honestly like to share those benefits with others? Forget about the money you make by having more students. Didn't you become an instructor and open a school to help others? Remember what was said at the beginning of the book. When your goal is to help and to serve others, fame and fortune will find their way to your door.

Most people who call your school want the same benefits that you enjoy as a black belt, except they don't know how to convey this request. Most prospective students have thought about taking lessons for years before mustering up the courage and determination to do something about it. Now that you know how important martial arts instruction is to the caller, you should do whatever is necessary to help the caller. Help callers take that all-important second step through your sales promotions. By doing so, you may be able to change their lives just by following a professionally designed script.

PERSONAL SELLING AND
COMMITMENT COUNSELING

PERSONAL SELLING AND COMMITMENT COUNSELING

pricing • payment • overcoming objections
counseling • sealing the deal

Public relations, advertising and sales promotions are used to inform and encourage prospective students to visit your school. Now that the prospect has arrived at your studio, the art of personal selling must be employed.

Individuals who want to participate in martial arts instruction are constantly bombarded by other recreational options. Martial arts instructors must compete with soccer, football and other sports instructors as well as an abundance of video games. They also must compete with other martial arts studios for students. To be successful, you must learn to sell your programs.

Until recently, the art of personal selling was not a popular subject among martial arts instructors. Many instructors believed that students would come if they were good teachers with good facilities. Unfortunately, there are many masters who retire each year with survival incomes because they never learn to properly sell their programs.

Without personal selling, your program will not reach its full potential. At first, many instructors might feel the same sort of anxiety with selling that others feel when performing CPR. By having a set routine and practicing, they can provide lifesaving routines without being overwhelmed by nerves. Successful selling can provide life support for your studio.

Another term to describe personal selling is commitment counseling. A recent study found that 18- to 30-year-olds view the term "selling" as undesirable. I use the term "commitment counseling" in seminars with college-aged students to disguise the fact that I am teaching the participant to sell. When you buy, you make a commitment. You counsel or advise the prospective client to make the right decision and take lessons at your school.

In Kenneth Blanchard's popular book, *The One Minute Manager*, the author explains that "selling" really means helping buyers get a good feeling about what they are purchasing. In order to ensure that buyers have a good feeling about the purchase they make at your school, the proper practitioner of personal selling should do the following:

Solve problems for the prospect.

Often, buyers lack a clear understanding of the programs that you offer and the methods you use to help them achieve their personal goals. Programs can be tailored to suit each individual.

Provide correct information.

By using a carefully laid-out presentation manual, you can show buyers exactly what they will be paying for and what they can reasonably expect to achieve.

Encourage the prospect to make a purchase that serves as an affirmative conclusion to the free classes and presentation.

Students come to your school because they might benefit from your instruction. When prospects come to your school, you will either motivate them to join your program or fail to satisfy their needs, causing them to walk out the door.

If you have a product or service that you have benefited from and believe in, it should be easy to encourage others to benefit from that product or service. When a student feels good about paying for lessons at your school, you have engaged in the practice of successful personal selling.

Qualifying the Prospect

The process for successful selling encompasses four areas:

1. Qualification of the Prospect

You must answer these two questions before determining what program will best suit the student: 1) How can I help the prospect, and 2) what can the person afford to pay for instruction? It is a natural instinct for a prospect to raise some objection about making a decision and spending money. When students are taking free introductory classes, take the time to learn what you can do to cater the selling approach specifically to them. This information will also help you determine how much they can pay for instruction.

2. Completion of the Free-Class Offer

During the free-class program, teach to the needs of the prospective student. Find out specifically why the prospect wants to take instruction and what his or her goals are. You will need this information to finish your sale.

3. Completion of the Presentation Manual

In an orderly and detailed manner, review the prospect's progress in the free-class program and present the prospect with specific information on choosing a program and a payment method.

4. Closing

Use the information that you collected during the qualifying process to assist the prospect in making an affirmative decision, then close the sale. Specific closing techniques will be discussed later.

If you follow the four-part sales program in detail, seven out of 10 students who enroll in your free class will most likely sign a contract to train at your school. Failure to complete any one of the four areas could result in a missed sale.

How to Set Prices for Specific Programs

In today's schools, programs are designed to provide specific results. Students no longer pay for a month at a time. The owner of an average full-time martial arts school charges close to $100 to $150 per month for instruction. The more months that a prospect signs up for, the less he or she should expect to pay for monthly instruction, so be flexible when designing program prices.

Several years ago, I priced my Green Belt Program at $999. I asked for a $150 down payment. I financed the remaining balance of $849 ($999 minus $150). The finance fee, or the price the prospect will need to pay for financing the program over time instead of immediately, was 10 percent of the balance or $85. (Nowadays, schools with a general enrollment of 60 students or more tend to use a financing company like the Educational Funding Company.) Then I divided the total, $934, ($849 plus $85) by 12 (for 12 months). The monthly payment came out to $77.83. I personally collected money from each student with a payment book. Monthly fees were sent to a post-office box designated as "Tuition Finance." As the undisclosed owner of the tuition finance company, I could send late notices and payment requests without damaging the teacher/student relationship. Today, I would simply hire one of the many successful tuition-collection companies.

Green Belt Program

$	999.00	Base Program Price
-	150.00	Minimum Down Payment
$	849.00	Remaining Balance
+	85.00	Finance Fee
$	934.00	Total Remaining Balance
/	12	Months
$	**77.83**	**Monthly Payment**

The student could decrease the monthly fee by increasing the down payment. For example, let's say a prospective student called my school and asked, "How much does it cost?" I would explain that some of my students pay as little as $35 per month (with a 50 percent down payment at registration), and others pay as much as $77.83 per month. In short, there are no set monthly payments. The student can choose the tuition that works best for his or her budget.

I priced my six-month Gold Belt Program at a higher per-month price. The Gold Belt Program price was $719 (approximately $120 per month). It was easy to see that the better value (an additional cost of just $279 for six additional months of instruction) was the Green Belt Program.

I never sold a Brown Belt Program. I only used the brown-belt rank as a reference point. The Brown Belt Program lasted 24 months and cost $2,399. There were no benefits or reduced prices. I wanted the student to know that the Brown Belt Program was very expensive. The Brown Belt Program was just there for comparison to the Black Belt Program.

Even with noticeable savings, I sold only a few Green Belt and Gold Belt Programs. Almost all my students contracted for the Black Belt Program. The Black Belt Program was designed for three years of instruction. However, it was paid for within 24 to 28 months. Although the potential cost was $3,600 ($100 x 36 months), I sold the Black Belt Program for $1,999.

Included in the program, the student received a free uniform, patch and membership in the AIKIA national organization for accreditation. After a down payment of $200 or more, the prospect had a finance fee of $179, which was added to the total. Essentially, the Black Belt Program came with added incentives and was priced to sell.

Black Belt Program
$1,999.00 Base Program Price
-   200.00 Minimum Down Payment
$1,799.00 Remaining Balance
+   179.00 Finance Fee (10% of $1,799.00)
$1,978.00 Total Remaining Balance
/   24 Months
$ 82.41 Monthly Payment
or
$1,999.00 Base Program Price
-   200.00 Minimum Down Payment
$1,799.00 Remaining Balance
+   179.00 Finance Fee (10% of $1,799.00)
$1,978.00 Total Remaining Balance
/   28 Months
$ 70.64 Monthly Payment

I told the students that after they achieved brown-belt (or red-belt) status, which takes about two years, they would be asked to serve as assistant instructors. They would not be charged for the last year if they became assistant instructors. Also, I let them know that once they achieved black belt, I would hire them to teach for me, and they could earn back the cost of their instruction. It was an offer that few refused. While many students signed up for the program, few tended to earn the rank of black belt. In addition, those that endured the tests for the rank made excellent instructors.

Even though the dollar difference between the Green Belt and Black Belt programs was a little less than $1,000, prospects believed that they were getting more because they received two additional years of instruction. To them, it was the better deal priced at what appeared to be only a few hundred dollars per year. And that's partly the reason that 90 percent of my students signed up for the Black Belt Program.

Many schools offer a basic six- to 12-month introductory program and then convince their students to upgrade to a belt system within the first year of the program. Typically, upgrades include more months of instruction and participation in private classes or specialty classes. It is common today to find schools where multiple arts are taught. Often, students pay for a base art and then upgrade their contracts to gain admittance in classes for additional arts.

The Contract or Promissory Note

The contract, sometimes called a promissory note, is used in most schools. The contract guarantees that the student will get to participate in a class taught by a professional martial artist in exchange for an agreed-on payment. The price agreed on at the time of the sale remains set and cannot be increased until the contract expires. The school contract is similar to a time-share property agreement. You are agreeing to pay for the use of a space in class. Whether you use it is up to you. To see an example of a successful contract, see Appendix B.

The most efficient way to collect tuition is to employ a professional martial arts billing company. If your contracts allow for electronic funds and transfer payments, then the tuition is deducted from the student's account. Tuition billing companies work for a 2 percent to 5 percent collection fee. In many cases, the billing company will provide business counseling as part of the school contract. Each month, you receive a check from the billing company for the amount of tuition collected, minus the collection fee.

Free Classes

Most owners of modern martial arts schools offer at least one free week of instruction. To create a positive impression during the free week, have an upbeat, experienced instructor run the trial lessons so the prospective student will be motivated to sign up for paid classes.

Here's some advice: When prospective students sign up for free classes, find out what their interests are so you can meet their needs during their trial period. Many students are interested in self-defense. Other students want weight loss and fitness, and some have the desire to compete in tournaments. Make it a point to answer questions even before they're asked. Remember, you are collecting information about each student. The plan is to motivate, entertain and educate the prospective student during the first week of instruction. By Wednesday of any given week, you should have several prospects asking, "How can I sign up?" When you think that they have sufficient information to make an informed decision, schedule a time to take them through the presentation manual.

There are three distinct benefits to offering the free-class program to all prospective students:

- The free class is designed so that the student becomes informed and excited about taking martial arts at your school.
- The free class gives the school owner the opportunity to determine how specific wants and needs can be met.
- The free class gives owners the chance to answer specific questions in a stress-free environment. The answers to the questions will be used in designing a program and in overcoming potential objections during the close.

The free-class program is a tried-and-trusted method for recruiting new students. Some schools have extended the free-class program to two free weeks. Other schools sell an introductory package that includes a karate gi, DVD, promotional items and a month of instruction for $39 to $69. They basically charge for the items being sold and provide the month of instruction at no additional cost. Experiment with each concept and decide what works best for you.

Presentation Manual/PowerPoint

If everything goes well, the prospect will be motivated to ask how he or she can join at the end of the week. Using a printed notebook, manual or a PowerPoint presentation, guide the student through the process of signing up for instruction. Invite the student into your office and shut the door to limit distractions. It helps to provide a visual while you discuss the program. The presentation manual provides the visuals. There are several points to follow:

Introduction

Have an introductory page with photos of at least one of the following: you, your staff members, your students or your facilities.

Credibility

List credentials, affiliations and organizations that provide accreditation for students taking instruction at your school.

Testimonials

List several popular questions, and provide specific answers. Some sample questions are: "Why practice martial arts?" "How long does it take to learn self-defense?" "What organization provides accreditation for instruction at your school?" and "Which style is best?"

Programs and Benefits

There is an old saying that goes, "You sell what you show." Consider including a belt chart. Next to each color belt, list the number of hours or months required to test for the rank color. Also, identify goals that the student can achieve at each rank. If you sell belt programs, identify three levels: beginner/gold, intermediate/green, and advanced/brown. Complete the display with information about the Black Belt Program.

In order to encourage students, many schools offer a "black-belt club." Typically, members of the club have purchased the school's most expensive program so they can work toward the goal of earning the coveted black belt. Black-belt club membership usually includes unlimited classes, prepaid belt exams, specialty classes and other perks associated with exclusive membership.

If you prefer to sell months or years of instruction, identify the term of instruction as your program. Many schools sell a simple one-year program. Independent clubs may prefer a semester or four-month program.

Payment Plans

After the student has a complete understanding of the programs that you offer, identify the cost associated with each program.

During the crucial time when a sale can either be won or lost, the presentation manual is your focal point. Take the time to present your case in a way that excites the buyer into purchasing one of your programs. And practice your presentation until it becomes a finely honed performance. By doing so, you can best help your prospect make a decision that is beneficial to your school but also for him or her.

The Big Picture

Remember to ask yourself, "Can I help this student?" and "What can this person afford to pay for instruction?" There is no reason to sell prospective students programs that they cannot afford. A college student who is home for the summer or a military soldier who is home on leave are poor prospects for one-year programs. A person who is out of work will be unduly burdened with a long-term contract. There are some individuals who do not qualify for instruction unless you offer your services for free.

Advertising and public relations inform potential members about your school and motivate them to visit it. Sales promotions provide incentive. The tour, free classes and presentations educate them. Despite your best efforts, though, many of your prospects will say no when asked to sign a contract for instruction.

In the martial arts business, when a customer says no, it usually means I have failed to qualify him or her. The negative is actually a request for more information. The prospect needs more answers before making an informed decision. Usually, a prospect says no because he or she is afraid of making a commitment or the seller failed to provide sufficient reasons to sign up.

Sales specialists are taught to initially interpret the word "no" as an objection. The prospect is not ready to say "yes." To help a prospect overcome his or her objections, have the answers prepared in advance. It is natural for the prospect to initially avoid agreeing to spend money. Most objections focus on the cost of training. During the qualifying phase, while the student is taking free classes, ask questions that will cover most objections. Objections can be traced to the following roots:

"I don't have time."

Prospects might say they do not have time to take lessons or that they are not available during the times posted for your classes.

"I don't have the money."

Prospects might confess that they do not have the money to pay for lessons.

"I need to ask someone else."

Sometimes, prospects note that they must ask someone close to them, such as their parents or spouse.

"I don't like the style/teacher/program."

After the free class, a few prospects might tell you that they did not like the program.

"Let me think it over."

Many students will use this excuse so they do not have to make a commitment.

The key to overcoming objections is to ask questions during the qualifying process while the prospect participates in the free-class program. Remember, a prospect's decision involves a purchase of several thousand dollars and at least a year. You need to have the answers to important questions regarding membership obligations in advance of the crucial sales presentation. Here's how:

Time

Ask the prospect these questions: "What days could you see yourself training? We have some students who train three to four times a week. Do you see yourself practicing that much?" By asking such questions, you discover whether the prospect has time to benefit from instruction. Travel time also comes into play. Most school members travel three to five miles to reach the studio. Make sure that travel time and distance will not interfere with instruction. Remember, ask these questions and receive an affirmative answer before you begin to show the client the presentation manual.

Money

During general conversation, ask the prospect questions like: "Do you work around here? Do you like it there?" This type of questioning provides information about the prospect's ability to pay for instruction. Before inviting the prospect to your office to discuss programs, be sure that money will not be a reason for refusal. Also mention to the prospective client that the average cost of lessons runs about $100 to $150 per month. Ask the client, "How does that sound to you?" Prepare the client for the price before you bring it up at closing time.

Ask Someone Else

Ask the prospect before, during or after class, "Who do you think is going to like it most when you learn martial arts? You? Your wife?" This line of questioning helps you determine whether the prospect needs to ask someone or can make the affirmative decision without consulting someone else.

Don't Like the Program/Style/Teacher

By now, you should be a pro at asking the right questions during the qualifying process. You will know during the free-class period whether the prospect likes the program. If you discover objections during the free-class program, resolve the issues before attempting to close the sale.

Remember, the student wants to take your classes and needs the benefits of your program. Also, it is natural for a prospect to initially balk at the cost of a program. As a shopper, you teach yourself to "shop" for the best price. You want to look around, think about it and visualize yourself using the product or benefiting from the service. You usually also take time to consider why you "may not" want to buy the product. You play "devil's advocate" with yourself. Still, you come to the conclusion to buy. Your prospect is going through the same process. By having an organized method, you can best serve your potential student.

Key Motivating Factors

People are motivated to take martial arts lessons for various reasons. Find out what motivates your prospective students and you will both save time and better serve your clientele. A school owner who promotes reality-based martial arts may find that his prospects are motivated by a focus on real-world situations. A traditional school owner may emphasize the culture, lineage and tradition of a style. An MMA school owner may emphasize the success of his fighters to attract new students. There are seven primary motivating factors for taking martial arts instruction:

1. Fitness/Pride

Students want to look and feel better in order to impress others. Many students enjoy martial arts movies and dream about being like the hero, who typically is in great physical shape and easily able to wow people.

2. Reducing Fear

For many people, self-defense is their primary reason for taking martial arts lessons. Living without fear is a goal for most.

3. Pleasing Others

Some people will sign up for lessons to make someone else happy. Many kids agree to take lessons not because they want to but because they want to satisfy the desires of their parents or grandparents.

4. Duty

Military, criminal justice and security personnel might need self-defense and fitness instruction to fulfill work obligations. Many recreational leaders and public-school teachers might feel more comfortable at their jobs if they knew how to defend themselves.

5. Revenge

The majority of martial arts movie plots are based on the theme of revenge, and some people take martial arts for the same reason. Fortunately, quality martial arts programs tend to make people more peaceful, not vengeful.

6. Profit

In some professions, martial arts instruction can lead to better-paying jobs. Actors, teachers and of course prospective martial arts instructors might gain profit from taking lessons at your school.

7. Character Development/Discipline

Many people who you will lead through your presentation manual are the parents and grandparents of kids who may enter your program. Character development may be of major importance to them.

Many of today's top martial arts instructors have at least 350 students enrolled per school. These professional instructors know what motivates their students to take lessons. They know that prospective students will hesitate when asked to sign contracts for instruction. They know that questions about time, money, approval, the program and the style are typical and should be addressed before the prospects enter the office.

As a school owner, I successfully closed the contract more than 90 percent of the time because I did not invite a prospect into my office to discuss programs, prices and contracts until I was certain that the person was perfectly qualified. I didn't learn this process overnight. I made many mistakes along the way. For example, I once let two students enter the office at the same time. Each had a separate objection. As soon as I isolated one objection, the other came up with a new objection. I quickly decided to reschedule their appointments rather than come off as a high-pressure salesman.

Closing the Deal

After presenting your program and asking the prospective student to make a decision, it is time to close the sale. "Closing" involves convincing a prospect to sign a contract and make an initial down payment. A good salesperson always looks for buying signals. For example, the prospect might pull out a credit card or checkbook. I always appreciate a prospect who asks questions because good questions can be interpreted as a buying signal. After only a few successful sales, you will begin to learn when your prospect is ready to close.

There are several standard closes that I find useful:

Test Close

Anytime you observe a buying signal, give a test close. A buying signal—like pulling out a credit card or asking whom to make the check out to—indicates that the prospect is ready to make a purchase. The test close is given in the form of a question, such as, "So, Mr. Jones, you look ready to pay for the program now?" Shake your head up and down, using affirmative body language.

Punch Close

This close ends with the word, "Right?" and the use of positive body language. Let's say that the prospect has asked about prices and contracts and has demonstrated a keen interest in getting started. You might give a statement such as, "You want to go for the Black Belt Program, right?" Shake your head in approval. Smile.

Alternate Choice

Provide two choices, and the prospect will select one. For example, say, "Which is better for you, Mr. Jones, the Monday class or the Tuesday class?" Or if a buying signal indicates that a purchase is about to be made, ask the prospect, "Did you want to use a check or credit card?" The alternate-choice close can be used to encourage a favorable response.

Three-Day Close

Sometimes a prospect is excited about your program but can't get past the "think it over" or "ask someone else" objections. You can write your contract to take effect in three days. The prospect can then write a check to be cashed three days later to coincide with the contract date. The three-day close also has been termed the "puppy-dog" close. Imagine that you don't want to make a commitment to own a dog, but a friend asks you to take a puppy home for the weekend while he is out of town. You play with the puppy. You feed him. He sleeps at the foot of your bed and nibbles at your toes in the morning. When the three days are over, you don't want to give the puppy back to his owner. The same thing happens when you send a prospective student home with a black-belt contract; the person is now part of your program and does not want to give it up. The three-day close is a low-pressure way to convince the student to sign up.

Higher-Authority Close

One objection might be, "I can't afford a down payment." Your response, using the higher-authority close, is to ask your boss for permission or a coupon to reduce the down-payment cost. For example, you can retrieve a $50 coupon to be given to the prospect for use as a down payment toward the contract at anytime. The use of a coupon or permission from your boss often provides a positive incentive to sign your contract. If you are the boss, it's easy to offer a discount for signing up.

Dollar-a-Day Close

This close also has been termed the "break it down to the ridiculous" close. Often, this close is an effective response to "It costs too much," or "I can't afford it." Let's say that you demonstrate that your program costs $900 per year. Explain to the prospective buyer that $900 actually breaks down to less than $3 per day.

Summary Close

Some salespeople prefer to summarize all the reasons for signing up at the end of the presentation.

Try to match the closing method to the buying signals presented by the prospect. Also, you can combine any of the closing methods. As you gain success as a martial arts salesperson and commitment counselor, you may create new closing methods or tailor the closing methods to specific markets. I knew a school owner who used the three-day close in 90 percent of his presentations. He taught in a college town and discovered that college students preferred the no-pressure feeling of the three-day close. His sign-up rate was very high.

Use a System to Overcome Objections

To be a successful salesperson, you have to become a successful listener. While you give your presentation, watch the prospective students. Observe any buying signals and, above all, listen to what they have to say. There are four stages to overcoming objections:

1. Listen and agree.

Often, counselors are taught to empathize with prospective clients. Phrases such as, "I can appreciate your concern," "I understand where you are coming from," or even a simple, "I see what you mean," can be used to show concern and help you prepare to overcome objections.

For example, at the end of your presentation, you typically ask the prospective student to sign the contract. The presentation might end with a phrase such as, "So, Mr. Jones, you would like the Black Belt Program, right?" Nod your head in an affirming manner. If there is an objection, then say nothing. Just listen.

After the prospect has provided an objection, agree with his or her comments. Repeat the objection to be sure that you understand it correctly. Say something such as, "I can appreciate your concern, Mr. Jones, that you feel like you need to talk this over with your wife." Then put your own spin on the objection.

2. Isolate the objection.

Isolate the objection to make sure that you have the correct one. Sometimes people say that they need to think it over when they are actually concerned about the money. You must determine the correct objection in order to successfully close the sale.

Remember, an objection is a request for more information. To help the prospect understand the nature of his or her objection, repeat the objection. Say something such as, "In other words, Mr. Jones, you like the program and you feel that you want the Black Belt Program. You just think you should check with your wife first. Is that correct?"

3. Set a condition.

At this point, you have isolated the objection. Now you must set a condition. Remember, if you did your job properly when you qualified the prospect, you already have the answer to the objection. Say, "You feel that if you talk it over with your wife, you would be certain that she wants you in the program. Is that correct, Mr. Jones?"

When doing this, recall clues that might have happened earlier. For example, maybe when you asked Mr. Jones what his wife thought about him taking karate lessons, he said that she had looked up the number and set the appointment for him. Say, "It sounds like your wife is in favor." The prospect will agree. He already knows that his wife is in favor. Remember that prospects have a natural tendency not to want to make a decision until they have all the information that they need.

4. Close.

You are ready to close for the second time. If you go for a second close, consider adding an incentive such as a three-day close, a higher-authority close or a summary close. Use the summary close if the prospect seems very interested. Consider the higher-authority close as an incentive or motivation for signing the contract now.

In summary, you made your presentation. The prospect raised an objection. You listened to the objection and agreed that he or she had a valid point. You repeated the objection with a spin to set a condition. If you agreed that the objection was simply a request for more information and you presented the missing information, the prospect will sign up for the program.

To make sure that your prospective student fully understands all the ramifications of signing the contract, follow the same formula (listen, agree, isolate, close) as many times as it takes. Do not badger, degrade or argue with a prospect. Collecting specific information during the qualifying process and following a specific presentation procedure will dramatically increase your chances for closing.

In many ways, the art of personal selling is similar to sparring. To win, you must know your opponent's strengths and weaknesses, be in shape mentally and physically, and have a game plan. Prepare for every possibility because sometimes you will face serious opposition and have to go with the flow, feed off your partner's energy and answer the offense with a superior countermove.

By the time the prospect is invited to sign a contract, he or she should be motivated to buy. You know exactly what you can do to help the prospective student and know what he or she can afford, how long he or she has wanted to take lessons, who will make the final decision, and which lesson time works best for the prospective student. Prospects come to your school because they want your program's benefits. Never take this responsibility lightly. As a professional instructor, you have a responsibility to provide a service to your clientele and help others. Learning and mastering the art of personal selling allows you to better fulfill those obligations.

CONCLUSIONS

In this book, I have outlined several concepts to ensure your success in running a martial arts business:

- develop the right product or service
- place your product in a favorable location
- offer your program at the most favorable price,
- promote your program by employing the principles and practices of advertising, public relations, sales promotions and personal selling and commitment counseling

The marketing practices outlined in the book will help you gain more students, serve more clients and increase your income substantially, but only if you put them into practice. If you don't, you won't receive the benefits.

When you get up each morning, the way you "dress to impress" is a form of advertising. At the dinner table, when you tell others about what you achieved that day, you engage in public relations. When you ask a person out for a date and you mention going out to eat at a fine restaurant, you are giving a sales promotion. Marketing is a dynamic concept, and those who achieve the most in life know how to do it effectively.

But the art of marketing is just as challenging as the art of teaching. As an instructor, you have a genuine desire to help students develop the skills that make the martial arts beneficial. Now that you have the skills to successfully promote your school and art, you can ensure that your students not only learn from your teachings but also feel like they have made a worthwhile investment.

Remember, instructors are measured by how much they give to others and not by how much they accumulate. In conjunction with your marketing skills, provide students with the finest instruction. Work to give them a school that supports them physically and mentally. Like the teachers of old, an instructor has a responsibility to balance the generosity of the martial arts master with the drive of the entrepreneur. By using your marketing skills to build up a school that you care about, you will create a bond with your students that ensures that they will always think of you as "the teacher."

APPENDIX A

National Self-Defense Awareness Survey

This survey was designed by AIKIA, a national martial arts and self-defense organization. AIKIA designed the survey to teach participants why they need self-defense. This survey will make them aware of the ways they may choose to defend themselves.

Please answer the following questions:

1. In your home, do you feel that you are:
   a) Very safe
   b) Sometimes safe
   c) Not safe

2. Do strange noises ever wake you up at night?
   a) Yes
   b) No
   c) Sometimes

3. In your neighborhood, do you feel safe?
   a) Very safe
   b) Sometimes safe
   c) Not safe

4. What makes you feel safe?
   a) Having a telephone present
   b) The presence of police
   c) A gun in the home

5. If you were alone and had no access to a telephone or police assistance, could you defend yourself?
   a) Yes
   b) Probably not

6. Imagine you are at an ATM. You are alone. A man is standing nearby, smoking a cigarette. It's dark. No one else is close by. Do you approach the ATM to get money?
   a) Yes
   b) No

7. How would it make you feel if you knew that you could defend yourself in any type of situation?
   a) Great
   b) I already feel like I can defend myself in any type of situation
   c) I don't know how I would feel

8. Have you ever considered taking martial arts lessons?
   a) Yes
   b) No
   c) I have taken lessons in karate/*taekwondo*/mixed martial arts/ *jujutsu*/kickboxing/other.

To thank people for participating in the survey, give them a coupon for two weeks of free instruction at your studio.

APPENDIX B

MARTIAL ARTS TUITION APPLICATION

_____   _____
Martial Arts School   Instructor

Name of Applicant_____ Date of Birth_____

Address_____

City_____ State_____ ZIP Code_____

Occupation_____ E-mail_____

Home Phone_____ Work Phone_____

Employer_____

Address_____

City_____ State_____ ZIP Code_____

Instruction Fee

Note (Installment)

$ _____ Down Payment _____ Date _____
I have reserved a space in the Martial Arts class. This space will not be resold, and so long as the contract is in force, I have guaranteed payment for that space. My failure to regularly attend class does not relieve me of the obligations, regardless of the circumstances, to pay the promissory note I have signed for $ _____, payable in _____ consecutive monthly installments of $ _____ due on the _____ day of each month beginning _____ (date) and each month thereafter until full amount is paid.

Signature _____

NOTICE OF CANCELLATION BY DATE _____

Although your contract clearly states that it is absolutely noncancelable, the Martial Arts Studio has requested that you be given a reasonable amount of time to review your financial commitment. Completing payments on a promissory note should be considered a serious matter that could affect your credit rating. Therefore, you may cancel this transaction at any time prior to midnight of the third business day after the date of this transaction or by 12 a.m. _____. Should the contract be canceled on or before this date, any funds exchanged as a down payment will be applied toward instruction at the rate of only $ _____ per month until such funds are depleted.

To cancel this transaction, mail a signed and dated copy of this cancellation notice or any other written notice to:

Address_____

City_____ State_____ ZIP Code_____

After 1 a.m. on this date _____, your contract goes into full force to be controlled by the collection service. Failure to pay installments after the 10th of any month in which a payment is due results in a 5 percent late charge. Should default be made in any monthly installment, the entire remaining sum shall be due and payable at the option of the owner of this note.

Accidents

It is further expressly agreed that all instruction, services, consultation and use of equipment and facilities shall be undertaken by Member at Member's sole risk, and Member assumes the risk for any such injuries or damage arising out of or in any way connected with his/her use of any of the services or facilities. Martial Arts Studio shall not be liable for any claim, demand, injury, expense, damage, action or cause of action, arising out of or connected with the use of any of the services or facilities of Martial Arts Studio, including those arising from acts of active or passive negligence on the part of Martial Arts Studio, its servants, instructors, agents or employees. Member, for himself/herself and on behalf of himself/herself, executors, administrators and assigns, does hereby expressly forever release and discharge Martial Arts Studio, its successors or assigns, as well as the officers, directors, employees, instructors, agents and consultants, from all such claims, demands, injuries, expenses, damages, actions or causes of action.

Further, Martial Arts Studio is not responsible for any loss or injury to personal property of Member while on, about, or as a result of being at Martial Arts Studio. Member agrees to abide by all rules and regulations adopted, including the time scheduled for instruction and use of the Martial Arts Studio as posted.

Signature _____ Date _____

ABOUT THE AUTHOR

Dr. Jerry Beasley is a professor of exercise, sport and health education at Radford University in Virginia where he has directed the martial arts program since 1973. He holds a doctorate in education administration.

As a martial artist, Beasley is a black belt in karate, *taekwondo*, *hapkido*, *jujutsu* and kickboxing. He has earned black belts from several *Black Belt* Hall of Fame members, including Joe Lewis, Michael DePasquale Sr. and Wally Jay. In 2000, Beasley was also inducted into the *Black Belt* Hall of Fame as Instructor of the Year.

In 1978, Beasley developed the American Independent Karate Instructors Association, which celebrated its 30th year in business in 2007. The association has certified more than 1,500 black-belt instructors. The organization's success led Beasley to develop the nation's premier martial arts training camp. Known simply as Karate College, the camp continues to attract martial arts enthusiasts, celebrities and instructors every year. It was recognized in 2008 with the *Black Belt* Industry Award for Best Seminar/Training Camp.

As a writer, Beasley has published more than 100 articles in popular martial arts journals. He is the author of eight books, including *Mastering Karate* (2002) and *The Jeet Kune Do Experience* (2001). Visit his Web site at www.aikia.net.

MORE from Black Belt Books

THE ULTIMATE GUIDE TO MIXED MARTIAL ARTS
by the Editors of Black Belt

Only one sport has reinforced elbow smashes to the head, flying knees and liver kicks. From MMA's controversial inception to its mainstream acceptance, from the iconic legacy of Rickson Gracie to the freakish knockout power of Chuck Liddell, from the unstoppable determination of Randy Couture to the emergence of tomorrow's champions, *Black Belt* has covered the sport's genesis and evolution. With *The Ultimate Guide to Mixed Martial Arts*, you will leap into the octagon with Chuck Liddell, experience the artery-crushing chokes of Rickson Gracie, devour Randy Couture's prescription for peak performance, master Dan Henderson's winning training methods and suffer the nasty takedowns of UFC bad-boy Tito Ortiz. A compilation of instructional articles and interviews with the industry's greatest champions, *The Ultimate Guide to Mixed Martial Arts* is the definitive resource on the athletes and techniques of the world's most intense and popular new sport. 216 pgs. (ISBN-13: 978-0-89750-159-0) **Book Code 488—Retail $16.95**

THE ULTIMATE GUIDE TO GRAPPLING
by the Editors of Black Belt

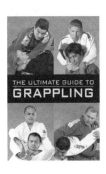

Attention, grapplers! This is the book you've been waiting for. From the arenas of ancient Rome to the mixed-martial arts cages of modern Las Vegas, men have always wrestled for dominance. Ground fighting is the cornerstone of combat, and *The Ultimate Guide to Grappling* pays homage to the art with three decades' worth of instructional essays and interviews collected from the archives of *Black Belt*. With more than 30 articles featuring legends like Mike Swain, John Machado, Gokor Chivichyan, Hayward Nishioka, Renzo Gracie, Bart Vale and B.J. Penn, you'll learn the legacy of Greek *pankration*, reality-based ground techniques for police officers and soldiers, the differences between classical *jujutsu* and submission wrestling and more! Transform your traditional art into a well-rounded and effective self-defense system today! 232 pgs. (ISBN-13: 978-0-89750-160-6) **Book Code 489—Retail $16.95**

THE ULTIMATE GUIDE TO STRIKING
by the Editors of Black Belt

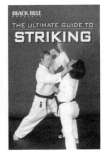

The Ultimate Guide to Striking examines striking techniques from various martial arts. Topics include *jeet kune do's* most efficient weapons, modern applications of *isshin-ryu* karate, vital-point attacks for women's self-defense, the vicious spinning backfist of *The Ultimate Fighter's* Shonie Carter, the "combat slap," *tang soo do's* lethal elbow strikes, the mysterious art of *mi zong* kung fu, Jeff Speakman's rapid-fire *kenpo* arsenal and more! Through scores of detailed photos and articles printed in *Black Belt* from 1990 to 2005, *The Ultimate Guide to Striking* provides a vast cultural and technical cross-section on the topic of striking. This collection is sure to be an enlightening and effective addition to any martial artist's training library. 248 pgs. (ISBN-13: 978-0-89750-154-5) **Book Code 483—Retail $16.95**

THE ULTIMATE GUIDE TO KNIFE COMBAT
by the Editors of Black Belt

More effective than a fist and more accessible than a gun, the knife is the most pragmatic self-defense tool. *The Ultimate Guide to Knife Combat* celebrates this simple, versatile, sometimes controversial weapon with essays and instructional articles written by the world's foremost experts, including Ernest Emerson, Hank Hayes, Jim Wagner and David E. Steele. *The Ultimate Guide to Knife Combat* presents an international cross-section of knife cultures and styles—from the heroic legacy of America's bowie knife to the lethal techniques of the *kukri*-wielding Gurkhas of Nepal—and features essential empty-hand techniques, exercises to improve your fighting skills, and advice on choosing the knife that's right for you. Spanning two decades of material from the *Black Belt* archives, *The Ultimate Guide to Knife Combat* provides everything you need to know about fighting with or against a blade. 312 pgs. (ISBN-13: 978-0-89750-158-3) **Book Code 487—Retail $16.95**

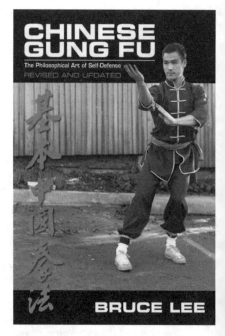